In the Shadow of His Hand

In the Shadow of His Hand

By
Sarah Margaret Smith

E-BookTime, LLC
Montgomery, Alabama

In the Shadow of His Hand

Copyright © 2006 by Sarah Margaret Smith

All rights reserved. No part of this book may be reproduced or transmitted in any form or by any means, electronic or mechanical, including photocopying, recording, or by any information storage and retrieval system, without permission in writing from the copyright owner.

Names of some of the persons within the text have been changed in respect for their privacy.

Library of Congress Control Number: 2006939159

ISBN: 1-59824-394-2

First Edition
Published November 2006
E-BookTime, LLC
6598 Pumpkin Road
Montgomery, AL 36108
www.e-booktime.com

The Scriptures within this book are taken from the King James Version of the Holy Bible unless otherwise indicated.

Acknowledgments

To those who have played an important part in the writing of this book, I give my heartfelt thanks – to my sister Alethia Alt, who compelled me to commence the project; to both my niece Kelly Fay and my friend Diane McKissack, who read and re-read the manuscript, helping me with everything from punctuation to the final layout; to my friend Peggy Kahler, who helped with the photos; to my sister-in-law Chris Brockles, for her ongoing encouragement; to Mr. Howard Prier, for his instruction in the book of Isaiah from which I took the title of my story; and, of course, to my dear husband Glenn, who has advised me, helped me, encouraged me and lovingly supported me in this undertaking.

Sarah Margaret Smith

Preface

At the insistence of my beloved husband Glenn, my sister Alethia, my sister-law Chris and a few close friends, I have been persuaded to write about my life and experiences. I'll not deny that my life has been somewhat different from the lives of most people, but isn't every life unique in its own way? I daresay anyone looking back over seventy-two years of their existence would have unusual stories to tell – some exciting, some sad, some humorous and some thought-provoking. Although my account includes some of the difficult times, it's not my purpose to write a "poor me" book but to encourage others to see a physical disability not as a tragedy but as a challenge with worthwhile lessons to be learned.

We live in a time when beauty, appearance and physical strength are highly rated, oftentimes above all else; but our physical being is only an insignificant part of who we are. By the grace of God, I've come to realize and appreciate His goodness and wisdom in giving me a life with physical challenges. All those years before I knew the Lord, I was unaware that I was *"in the shadow of His hand,"* unaware of His protection over me and that the difficulties of my life would be used to prepare me for future purposes.

Initially, my sister Alethia wanted me to write specifics about the polio epidemic, what I went through when polio first hit me, and how it has affected me. Chris wanted me to chronicle the humorous experiences. Others have wanted me to write a book about my spiritual journey. As I began, however, I realized that in order to give a true picture of my life I would have to touch on all its

vii

complexities. The physical, the mental, the emotional and the spiritual are intertwined and cannot be separated one from the other without giving a distorted view.

While this is only a mini-autobiography and certainly doesn't include every detail and event of my life, I've tried not to be biased in my own favor, as tempting as that may be. It hasn't been easy revealing some of the blotches on my character, but the One who knows all would frown on my being less than honest.

"... In the shadow of His hand hath He hid me, and made me a polished shaft; in His quiver hath He hid me."

Isaiah 49:2

The Title

The title of the book, *In the Shadow of His Hand*, is taken from a passage in Isaiah Chapter 49, verse 2. In this verse, the pre-incarnate Messiah is speaking figuratively of Himself being in the shadow of His Father's hand, hidden there until the time when He would be brought forth to accomplish His work of redemption on the cross, and ultimately to establish His kingdom. Similarly, those for whom Christ died are protected and kept in the shadow of the Father's hand for future purposes and acts of service unto the Lord.

Chapter 1

I was born in 1934, during the Great Depression. I was the youngest of five children. My father, Andrew Brockles, was a Greek immigrant who settled in Dallas, Texas, where he met my mother, Ola Feltnor, an American girl from Arkansas of Scotch-Irish and German descent. He was 26 and she was 16 when they married.

I don't remember times being particularly hard for us, although they may have been. We seemed to have everything we needed. With a swing set in the backyard, a new doll each Christmas, a pair of roller skates to take me up and down the block, and trees to climb, what more could I want? Of course, my dad worked long hours seven days a week at the downtown café that he and my uncle owned.

We lived in a three-bedroom white frame house in a modest neighborhood until I was twelve. With my sisters in one bedroom and my brothers in another, I slept in my parents' bedroom in the baby bed for years until my head pressed against one end and my feet against the other. After my older sister married, I was given the privilege of sharing the front room with my sister Alethia.

We went everywhere together as a family. There was no such thing as hiring a babysitter. Summer evenings after supper we would usually sit awhile on the front porch.

When the other children of the neighborhood came out, we'd catch lightning bugs or play hide-'n'-seek until time for our favorite radio programs. Life was simple and comfortable.

I remember my dad taking me shopping one day when I was about three. He bought me a dress, and I even got to wear it home from the store. It was a beautiful, brightly colored cotton print. Mama called it a dirndl dress.

Shopping with my dad

In the Shadow of His Hand

World War II interrupted this idyllic scene, however, and families huddled around their radios to listen to the news reports. I was frightened when my older brother went off to the army, afraid I'd never see him again, and greatly relieved when he came home safe and sound. Patriotism ran high and people saved their money to buy US War Bonds.

With everyone else older, wiser and more experienced, I usually just sat and listened to all the adult conversation. In fact, I became an ardent observer of life from about the age of three, watching my brothers and sisters growing up ahead of me. I was enthralled when my sister Sophie Mae would apply makeup. I'd sit on the floor next to the dressing table and take careful account of each step of the process. I remember my sister Alethia learning to walk in high heels and my brother Arge starting to shave. Being the youngest, I was the tag-along and could hardly wait to grow up.

There was music, singing, teasing and laughter in our household, along with the normal squabbles and fights typical of siblings. While our Dad was the more serious parent, always instructing and advising us to work hard and do right, Mama had a keen wit and enjoyed our crazy antics, often joining in with our fun. She helped us see humor even in the mishaps of life. After scraping a knee, for example, she would doctor it, give a quick hug and say, *"Don't cry. It'll get well before you marry!"*

The Saturday matinée at the neighborhood Arcadia Theatre was a treat for us kids. With the movie, of course, there would be a cartoon and an exciting Western serial that kept us on the edge of our seats and always ended with a cliffhanger. It was a quarter well spent.

My dad would ride the streetcar to and from work twice a day. He would leave early every morning in time to serve the breakfast and lunch crowds, come back home in the afternoon to rest and then return to the restaurant for the dinnertime rush. On hot summer days, he would stretch out in one of the striped canvas and wooden lawn chairs outside in the shade, and Mama would place pieces of ice wrapped in napkins on his forehead and his wrists. I would reluctantly lie down on the bed next to the open window in the back bedroom and hope for a cool breeze. Actually, I did enjoy that quiet time. Sometimes, Mama would come and lie beside me for a little while. She would sing or recite a poem. I would look out at the sky and the trees, carried away in my imagination as I listened to her. Then, I'd lie there alone quietly thinking about all kinds of things. In our modern world today with cell phones, iPods, CD players and television, it seems that the joy of quietness has been lost.

After his rest, before my dad went back to work, we would enjoy some family time all together. Mama would serve coffee and a snack, usually a sweet roll or buttered toast with honey. Sunday was usually the only time my dad had dinner with us at home, and everyone was expected to be there. We knew not to ask to leave the table until we were excused. Each of us would then get up, kiss both our parents, and go on our way to play.

We were privileged to have the experience of two cultures – the American and the Greek. Although Mother was only 16 years old when she married my father, her own American heritage flowed deep in her veins. Even so, she had a strong sense of responsibility to adapt to the customs of her husband, and she did so successfully. She and my father strengthened and complemented each other. Perhaps it was because underneath the different customs and traditions, they had basically the same values and priorities.

In the Shadow of His Hand

The Brockles Family, Christmas 1942

Somehow our parents knew how to handle little children. They weren't about to put up with bratty behavior or whining and pouting. We received the needed spankings in our early training, so that by the time we started school we knew we'd better behave. A piercing look from either parent was enough to strike fear in our hearts and straighten us up quickly.

My parents gave parties often, inviting other Greek families. Lots of food, usually lamb, pastitso, mousaka, and other Greek favorites were served along with retsina wine and ouzo (a licorice tasting liquor). We kids learned early about showing hospitality and were expected to help Mama in the preparations. One time my dad rebuked me sharply for sitting down in the living room to await the guests while Mama was still in the kitchen. *"But, Daddy, I finished all I know how to do,"* I replied in defense. *"Then go watch your mother and learn!"* he commanded.

We had a large mahogany Victrola, the wind-up kind, which stood in the corner of the dining room. Later, my older sister bought a real jukebox. I was always fascinated watching it light up and automatically drop a selected record onto the turntable.

Our first automobile was purchased in 1940. My dad scared us all to death while he was learning to drive. We soon learned that driving was not Daddy's forte. He did finally get the hang of it, at least enough to get a license. Our family vacations were often just a last minute decision for us to spend a few days at Galveston Island. He would call home from the restaurant to tell Mama, *"Ola, get packed. We're going to Galveston."* With less than two hours notice we were on our way, happy and excited, in spite of the six-hour long hot drive with no air conditioning! I always had to fight carsickness brought on by my excitement, the heat and also by my fear of Daddy's driving. We'd hold our breaths every time he tried to pass a car on that old narrow two-lane highway. After the long hot drive we would check into a tourist cottage facing the water, put on our swimsuits and head for the beach. I would float around in a rented inner tube while everyone else swam or jumped the waves. One time I got too far out and a huge wave crashed over me, pulling me off the inner tube and under the water. The water was deep and, not knowing how to swim, I just held my breath and closed my eyes tight. The next thing I knew I was washed up safely onto shore. Looking around for comforting words from family members, I found they were totally unaware of the incident. This life-threatening experience gave me a healthy respect for the ocean, and I never ventured far out again.

It was a great experience for me and my brother to spend a week or two in the summer with our Grandmother Feltnor who lived on a farm in East Texas. We learned to feed the chickens and gather eggs, and even tried to churn butter. There were two or three milk cows, a couple of hogs, a mule, a dog and two or three cats. On one of our visits, the sow had just delivered a litter of piglets. I couldn't resist going into the pigpen one day, even though Grandma told me not to. When I tried to pick up one of the baby pigs, the big Mama sow chased me out of the pen. I tripped over a piece of barbed wire, cutting a big gash in my ankle. I probably should have had stitches and a tetanus shot, but Grandma simply washed it out with turpentine and wrapped a rag around it. I still have the scar. We had to take our baths in a wash tub in the kitchen. Grandma would draw water from the well outside and heat it on the wood-burning kitchen stove. My least favorite thing was using the "out house." The stench, along with the flies and wasps darting in and out, kept my visits there from lasting any longer than absolutely necessary.

***

Dallas was a small city then – a little over four hundred thousand. It was a bit more cosmopolitan than neighboring Fort Worth. We had the Dallas Opera, the Dallas Symphony Orchestra, the Starlight Operettas and the Dallas Museum of Art. Mama saw to it that we attended a cultural event periodically. Several shopping centers had sprung up after WWII, but malls were non-existent. Ladies wore dresses, high heels and hats for downtown shopping.

College football was big in the late '40's and early '50's. With Doak Walker playing for SMU and drawing large crowds, the Cotton Bowl was expanded to seat 75,500. Daddy bought season tickets for the whole family even though he didn't understand much about the game, nor did I.

After the war, the restaurant business boomed and we moved to a larger house. Mama was happy to have more closets and more than one bathroom, and I, at last, had my own bedroom. We were a big close family. Even after my two sisters and older brother married, they lived nearby and were constantly coming over to our house.

I learned to drive when I was thirteen. After accomplishing backing out of the garage and down the driveway, I was pleasantly shocked when my dad gave me permission to drive his Cadillac up the street to my girlfriend's house. I could barely see over the steering wheel, and that first outing resulted in my backing into a tree. Thankfully, the small dent in the bumper wasn't noticed and I never confessed to causing it. There were no Drivers Education courses given at school at that time and licenses were seldom checked, so I drove without one for almost three years.

As my parents were becoming active in the AHEPA, a Greek-American organization, we began attending the state and national conventions each summer. Greek families from all of the country would attend. There were parties and activities for the young people while the older people attended meetings and their own social events. We drove down to Miami for the 1949 convention which included a short cruise to Cuba. This was before the Castro regime took over that island country. We saw all the sites and I was able to practice my high school Spanish. Afterwards, as we started driving home, a hurricane came blowing across Florida. Thankfully, my brother was old enough to do the driving. We tried to outrun it but it caught up with us just outside of Athens, Georgia. We took shelter in an old airplane hangar where we waited out the storm. I was totally oblivious to the dangerous capabilities of a hurricane and

In the Shadow of His Hand

spent that time in the car writing in my diary about the convention and the new friends I had met.

Vacations were fun but it was always good to get back home.

The Christmas just before my 14th birthday, my parents gave my sisters Sophie and Alethia, my sister-in-law Chris, and me brand-new electric Singer sewing machines. We all decided to take a six-week sewing course together. I was enthusiastic about learning but felt somewhat out of place with the three of them, since they were all "great with child" at the time. They made maternity clothes but I chose a lavender cotton material and a peasant style dress pattern, envisioning myself in it looking as glamorous as Kathryn Grayson in the movie *Showboat*. However, after almost sweating blood over every ruffle, it turned out to be the ugliest dress I'd ever seen. When I tried it on and stood before the mirror, even Mama said I looked like I had just gotten off a boat all right – but not the *Showboat!* I never wore the dress but at least I'd learned to sew, something young ladies were expected to know back then.

Chapter 2

By the summer of 1950, I was enjoying good times with friends and going to parties. As a sixteen-year-old, I was centered in on myself and my own pleasures – shopping for clothes, primping at the mirror and talking on the phone. Looking back, I realize that sixteen was much too young to be dating but my parents allowed it, although reluctantly. I would often have to plead and beg until they gave in. I'm ashamed to say that sometimes, when my pleading had no effect, I would devise a deceptive plan to have my boyfriend meet me at my girlfriend's house. My thinking? *"If other girls my age can date, I should be allowed to date. After all, Mama married when she was sixteen!"* Oh, how easy it was for me to try to justify the sins of my youth!

I was an average student, spending as little time as I could get by with studying or doing my homework. Piano was my only earnest endeavor. It was my entertainment, my conveyance into dreamland and my solace when I was troubled. After school I would race to get to the piano before my brother. Otherwise, he would pound out a few memorized boogie-woogie pieces over and over until Mama would make him stop.

My teacher, Miss Schawe, had never married but was devoted to teaching music. Her face was much like a female version of Ludwig Van Beethoven himself, austere and intense. She wore old-fashioned black dresses with white frilly lace collars. Her gray hair was usually a mess and she wore no makeup. In fact, she gave me a disapproving look when I began to wear lipstick. On the way to my lessons I would madly go over each note of my music, not wanting to displease my teacher! She would have preferred my spending more time perfecting my technical skills, but I played because I loved music, not because I had any desire to win competitions or to make piano a career. Having studied since age five, it had become a part of who I was. On Saturdays I would often go downtown to the Whittle Music Company where I would spend my allowance on all kinds of sheet music – classical, semi-operatic pieces and popular songs of the day. Then, I'd hurry home to play them. My family loved to sing, and they would gather around and harmonize to the old and new ballads while I accompanied on the piano.

I was looking forward to my senior year in high school, not because of the senior activities, but because I was eager to get out of school. My parents, knowing my boyfriend and I were getting serious, were glad when Chris invited me to go with her and her two children to Chicago on the train to visit her family for a couple of weeks. Because of the war in Korea, the train was crowded with soldiers. Maria was almost two years old and young Andrew was about nine months. I slept with Maria in the upper bunk and Chris slept with the baby – that is, we tried to sleep. But we enjoyed ourselves in Chicago. Chris's teenage cousins were eager to teach me to play tennis. I was embarrassed for them to see my lack of athletic ability, but we had lots of laughs anyway. Chris's mom stuffed us with all kinds of delicious Greek food, and I gained all the way up to 109 pounds!

Early Summer of 1950

    When we got back to Dallas things were very busy. Foolishly, I determined to lose those extra pounds I'd gained

In the Shadow of His Hand

by almost starving myself and continued playing tennis in spite of the hundred-degree weather. My brother Arge returned from his summer in Greece, looking and talking like an immigrant, and my parents were in the process of having a new home built. While Mother was in the midst of deciding on wallpaper and carpeting, as well as supervising us as we helped box up books and dishes, I began feeling sick with what we thought was the flu. Mother doctored me with a mustard plaster on my chest and placed the vaporizer filled with tincture of benzoin, a vile smelling potion, on the night stand. She placed a tent of newspapers over it so that I could breathe more of the potent fumes. The very next evening, we had a welcome home party for my brother but I stayed upstairs in bed. By the next week I felt better and was glad to be up and about.

Nick, a friend from church, called and invited me to go out with him, his girlfriend and another friend, who was in town for a few days. Steve was an 18-year-old soldier stationed in San Antonio, awaiting orders to be shipped out to Korea. The plan was to go to *Louann's,* a popular place for dancing. I had never been there but, surprisingly, my parents allowed me to go. They knew Nick well and, after all, since both he and Steve were Greek, my dad felt comfortable about it. Mainly, they were glad for me to see someone other than the boy I was so crazy about.

I wore a navy blue cotton dress and white ballerina shoes. The mambo was a new dance craze and Steve taught me the steps. Half way through the evening, I began to feel weak and feverish. I was embarrassed to admit that I was sick, but by ten o'clock I knew I had to go home.

My parents had gone out for the evening. Sick and frightened, I climbed into their bed and telephoned my sister-in-law. *"Chris, I'm sick. I think I've got polio!"* She stayed on the phone with me, trying to ease my fears, until I heard my parents drive up.

***

Polio – the dreaded word during those epidemic years. Swimming pools were closed and people were advised to avoid crowds. The number of cases climbed extremely high during the summer months and many died. Vacation time was approached with a sense of foreboding, although most families cautiously tried to continue their activities as normally as possible. Children were the hardest hit, but many adults also contracted the disease.

From the age of 8, I began to fear dying. My godfather's funeral was the first I remember attending. I was distressed by the black veils and mournful sobs of his wife and daughters, along with the chanted prayers over and over which my father explained were petitions to God to forgive the sins and accept the soul of my godfather into heaven. Death seemed dark and frightening and I hated the thought of it. I was particularly afraid of dying from polio because a young neighborhood boy just my age had died from it. I tried to push this fear to the back of my mind, but it disturbed me summer after summer. I had the feeling that someday the disease would get me. My brothers and sisters seemed to have none of those concerns, and I never discussed such things with them, nor with my parents. I remember one night, a few months before I got sick, standing before the full-length mirror in my bedroom, staring at my legs, my arms and hands, wondering and marveling at how they moved and functioned. I saw them as miraculous appendages that only temporarily belonged to me. Was this a hint of premonition? I don't know. Those who fear can imagine all kinds of disasters befalling them.

In the Shadow of His Hand

God says in His Word,

Whoso hearkeneth unto me shall dwell safely,
and shall be quiet from fear of evil.
Proverbs 1:33

Although we attended church fairly often, there was no family Bible reading or instruction given at home. The future was a scary mystery. I often wondered about God, but my wonderings only resulted in unfounded speculation. I had no resource to keep me *"quiet from fear of evil."*

When my parents arrived home, my fever was raging. Mother concluded that I was having a relapse of the flu. She stayed with me through the night, giving me aspirin and putting cool wet cloths on my forehead. The nausea, vomiting, fever, severe neck pain, and the inability to raise my head off the pillow continued the next day. My sister Alethia came over to help take care of me. Our family doctor came to the house (doctors made house calls back then), and after examining me he explained, *"Margaret, we must put you in the hospital to take some tests."* Our friend Wendell Merritt, whose family owned a funeral home and ambulance service, was called. I remember him carrying me down the stairs and putting me on the stretcher, but I have only a faint recollection of the ambulance ride to the hospital.

The spinal tap confirmed that I had contracted poliomyelitis.

Chapter 3

Nurses were scarce, many refusing to work because of their fear of polio. My sisters, Alethia and Sophie, and sister-in-law Chris took shifts staying with me. They were instructed to bathe, wash their hair and to remove and wash all their clothing as soon as they got home, for fear their children or others might contract the disease. With the diagnosis definite, it was mandatory that I be transferred by ambulance to the County Hospital to be quarantined.

The ambulance came to an abrupt halt. *"Where am I?"* I asked, but no one seemed to hear. *"Mama? Daddy? Where are you? Where are these men taking me?"* My mind cleared enough to remember being in the hospital. *"So, where could they be taking me now?"* I pondered. *"I must have died from polio, and now they're taking me to the morgue."* The stretcher on which I was lying was rolled out and quickly pushed into a building and down a long corridor. Another man rushed up along side and took my hand. It was my older brother. *"Andrew, where are they taking me?"* But he didn't answer. *"Andrew, am I dying?"* Then I realized that my words were only in my mind. I was moving my lips but I was too weak to speak aloud. Whether I was dead or alive, I didn't know. As we approached the end of the corridor, double doors were opened and two

16

In the Shadow of His Hand

nurses took me into the Isolation area. My brother was not permitted to follow. My confusion would have devastated me, but at this point I had no strength to react with any emotion. I slipped in and out of delirium. Finally, I managed to call out for my mother as I was being lifted onto a bed. A nurse, wearing a mask, began taking my vital signs and explained that none of my family could come with me. Later, I learned that I had been transferred to the Dallas County hospital to be kept in quarantine.

With total separation from family and the life that I knew, I felt suspended in a timeless vacuum. The present was a moment by moment experience of pain and helplessness. I was at the mercy of strangers – doctors who came to my bedside to observe me and nurses who tended me. Their faces were solemn and their tone serious as they discussed my case. The thought of paralysis had not yet reached my understanding, even though I lay motionless. I began to sense that the chief concern of the medical team was whether or not I would pull through.

The isolation unit was overloaded. I shared a room with three other polio patients – a young mother, a five-year-old little girl who cried continually and a 26-year-old man, a soldier who had just returned from Korea. White curtains were drawn around our beds when privacy was needed. Although my bed was near the window, only an occasional breeze gave relief during those hot days in August. My skin had become tender as if sunburned and even the weight of a sheet on my legs was painful.

On the second day, I was allowed one five-minute visit with a minister or priest. My father, determined to see me, passed himself off as the priest's assistant and came to my bedside. After that, he would come to the hospital in the afternoon and stand outside the building looking up at the window of my room. The nurse would wave to him but I was unable to see out. Just knowing my dad was there gave me a momentary remembrance of family and of being loved.

Because of the shortage of nurses, a young male medical student attended me. My parents didn't like the idea of my having a male nurse, but they had no choice. Monty was compassionate and dedicated to learning all he could about poliomyelitis. He persuaded the doctors to put me in an iron lung as my impaired breathing was preventing me from sleeping. The thought of being imprisoned in the large cylinder tank was frightening but once I was locked in, the compression and de-compression of the machine gave me the steady deep breaths I needed.

The Spirit of God has made me,

and the breath of the Almighty gives me life.

Job 33:4 NKJ

Aware of the seriousness of my condition, Monty was frightened for me. He suggested that maybe we should pray. *"I really don't know how to pray,"* he confessed, *"but I can say the Lord's Prayer."* So, he did. I followed along, whispering the words I had memorized as a young child.

A significant aspect of illness is that it brings one to a profound awareness of helplessness. Many live their lives thinking proudly, *"I am the Captain of my ship and the Master of my fate,"* but in reality we have no real control over sickness, health, life or death. My parents' love, concern or money was not able to make me healthy, and the doctors' knowledge and skills were not able to cure me; even my own desire to be well couldn't make me well. So, what is left and to whom can we turn but to God? Often, even a hardened unbeliever in dire circumstances will mutter a "foxhole" type prayer. Likewise, my acknowledgment of the Almighty at this time, of course, wasn't true faith in Him. Rather, it was merely a fatalistic assessment of His providence – whatever will be, will be; so, accept it. I didn't cry out in hope of His mercy because I didn't know Him as the God of mercy and grace.

The Lord takes pleasure in those who fear Him,

in those who hope in His mercy.

Psalm 147:11 NKJ

After a week in the iron lung, I graduated to a rocking bed for several hours each day. Its head-to-toe motion also enabled me to inhale and exhale more easily. My fever subsided and speaking became less exhausting.

A few days later, Miss Trent, a physical therapist, began coming by twice daily to give stretching exercises. Before the stretching, hot packs were wrapped around my arms and legs for about thirty minutes. These were wide strips of a thick flannel-type material that were soaked in very hot water then pushed through a wringer. As they cooled, they were replaced with hot ones. After the initial shock, the warmth was quite soothing. However, Miss Trent was a cold, heartless woman who seemed to delight in inflicting pain. Each of us in the ward learned to recognize her footsteps whenever she came down the hall. *"Here she comes,"* we would whisper, dreading the treatment. Even the young war hero who had survived two airplane crashes in the war would cry out with each torturous exercise. Monty, greatly disturbed by the painful treatment we were suffering, questioned Miss Trent. She, of course, insisted that the treatment *had* to be rigorous. After hours of research in the medical library, Monty brought books to my bedside to show me pictures of polio patients who had never received physical therapy. Their bodies were twisted and deformed. He tried to make me see the necessity of the stretching. Maybe I would have been willing to consider the benefits had it not been for Miss Trent's vindictiveness. She would command, *"If you yell out again, I'll give you five more minutes of stretching. Then you'll learn to be quiet!"*

By the second week, I was allowed an occasional brief visit with just one family member at a time. I would tell them how much I hated the physical therapy but they tried to encourage me to endure it, never realizing just how bad it really was. Regardless, there was no way they could transfer me to another hospital until I had passed what was considered to be the contagious stage. I kept asking to see my boyfriend but Mother wouldn't hear of it. One afternoon, however, my dad brought him to see me.

After twenty-one days, Miss Trent announced that I was going to sit up on the side of the bed. Without explaining how this sudden change of position might affect me, she abruptly pulled my legs over and lifted me up to sitting position. Immediately, I felt I couldn't breathe. My vision became blurred. I tried to speak, to scream out for help, but I couldn't. With her hand at my back to balance me, she nonchalantly chatted with one of the nurses. I was convinced I was dying and yet I couldn't get her attention. With my last bit of strength, I managed to lean forward and I actually bit her on the shoulder as hard as I could! It seems that all the hatred I had for this woman was released in that bite. Monty walked in just as this happened and pried my

In the Shadow of His Hand

teeth apart. Miss Trent stormed out of the room as Monty gently laid me back down on the bed.

The realization of what I had done put me into a state of panic. What would she do to me now? I begged Monty to call my doctor.

That afternoon Dr. Cox stood at my bedside. He announced that I was to be moved out of Isolation to another room where I would continue my physical therapy. The tears I'd been too weak to shed suddenly gushed forth and I pleaded my case against the wicked Miss Trent. *"I'll speak to her,"* Doctor Cox promised sympathetically. *"Oh, no! She'll be even meaner to me if she knows I said anything about her. Please, please, take me out of here today!"* I begged. *"Please, don't let her see me again!"* That afternoon I was transferred by ambulance back to the other hospital.

I was given a private room. My classmates sent lots of stuffed animals, cards and balloons. At last, my family and a few friends were allowed to visit daily. My boyfriend came to see me several times but Mother made him feel unwelcome. She informed his mother that I needed to concentrate on getting well and that his visits didn't help me. Oh, how I resented my mother for that, but realized a few years later that she was just afraid he would break my heart. The last time he came to see me I gave him back his ring that I had been wearing. It was an emotional time for both of us. I knew I couldn't fight my mother any more. Also, I knew he would be going off to college, and it was hardly fair to expect him not to date other girls. Also, deep down inside I think I was afraid he might eventually want to break up with me, and that would hurt too much.

I must have been a pitiful sight. My weight had dropped to 67 pounds. My first glimpse of myself in a mirror was startling. Each visitor who saw me, trying to be

Sarah Margaret Smith

positive, could only say, *"Well, Margaret, your color is good."* It became quite a joke with me and my family. They would tease me and say, *"Wow! Your color sure is good today!"* If it hadn't been for their sense of humor, I might have sunk into a morbid depression. Mother would put a pretty gown on me and try to fix my hair, but I still felt gaunt and unattractive.

Being back at the hospital in Dallas was a relief in most respects. The nurses were kind and attentive. My skin was no longer sore to the touch, and being turned was less painful. But early one morning after being positioned on my side, I lay there alone in the quiet when suddenly I saw a large white rat climb up and onto the top of the table adjacent to my bed. It was coming right toward my face and I couldn't move. I let out a scream that brought the nurses running and sent the rat scampering. After that I found it hard to fall asleep at night!

When I was informed that physical therapy would begin again, I was filled with anxiety. Thankfully, the therapy proved to be gentle, but because of the trauma I had been through, I continued to fear each treatment. Whenever I heard the gurney being rolled down the hall to my room, my heart would pound and I would almost throw up what little breakfast I had managed to eat. The stretching was given gradually and only up to the point of pain. The therapist, a chubby middle-aged woman, was kind and actually a bit too sympathetic. When she first met me, she burst into tears and blubbered, *"Oh, you poor dear!"* Each time she saw me after that she would slowly shake her head as if she'd never seen such a hopeless case. I couldn't help but be amused at her lack of professionalism.

Oddly enough, the thought of paralysis still had not sunk into my mind. I thought I was just weak from having been so sick. I was puzzled when the doctor said,

"Margaret, you've got to fight this!" Fight? How? I was trying hard to move my arms and legs but they wouldn't move.

The days and the nights dragged on. I waited and wondered when I would get well.

Illness is a solitary experience. We enter into a realm where no one, not even our loved ones, can go with us. They might be genuinely sympathetic as they try to cheer and comfort us, but the affliction is solely our own. As the old spiritual that Mama used to sing goes, *"Nobody knows the trouble I've seen, nobody knows but Jesus."* For the believer in Christ, such oneness with the Lord during an affliction is a special time of sweet communion with Him, unlike any other. However, as one of the Lord's lost sheep whom He would draw to faith many years later, I was quite alone.

When my dad would visit, he would stand at the foot of my bed and try to get me to press my feet against his hand. Suddenly, one day I was able to bend the big toe of my right foot, and everyone rejoiced at that improvement. As the days went on, I gained a little movement in my feet and my left hand. If someone bent my arm for me, I was able at last to scratch my nose!

Eating was still a problem. I had no appetite. My dad would send a tray of delicious food every day from our family restaurant – roast chicken, steak, baked potato. The nurse would stand over me aiming a fork of food at my mouth coaxing me to eat but I would take only a few tiny bites. The only thing I could get down was apple pie with vanilla ice cream. I survived on that dessert!

Chapter 4

By the beginning of October, the doctors suggested to my parents that they take me to Warm Springs, Georgia. The polio rehabilitation facility there was purported to be the best in the country. The 90-degree mineral springs flowed out from the hillside of Pine Mountain, and for years people had flocked there to bathe in the mineral waters. In 1924, Franklin D. Roosevelt visited the popular resort because of his own paralysis due to polio. He felt he benefited from the natural springs and wanted other polio patients to be helped. He bought the property and established the Georgia Warm Springs Foundation in 1927. Arrangements were made for me to go there, but I was concerned when I overheard that a room would cost $15.00 a day! A lot of money back then. Like most people in 1950, we were without hospitalization insurance but, thankfully, my dad was able to meet the cost.

I was discharged from the hospital in Dallas in late October. My family again called on Wendell to transport me and, as a special surprise, asked him to make a short stop-off at Harrell's Drugstore on the way home. It was a beautiful fall day. In contrast to the drabness of the hospital, the colors of the sky, the trees and foliage were vibrant. It was like going from a black and white movie to one in Technicolor! Although a bit apprehensive about leaving the

In the Shadow of His Hand

next day for Georgia, I was happy to see my familiar neighborhood as we drove along. School had just let out, and my friends were gathered at Harrell's, as usual. I felt self-conscious being rolled in on a stretcher, but everyone crowded around me and wished me well. It was quite a surprising send-off.

I hadn't seen our new house since its completion. Quite different from our English two-story, it was a sprawling ranch style. Mother led the tour as I looked about from the low stretcher. I felt dwarfed as we entered the large, high-ceilinged living room. Everything was lovely. And there was my grand piano, like an old friend waiting for me. *"Oh, let* me *go to the piano,"* I asked. *"I just want to touch the keys!"* I actually thought I would be able to play a little. Andrew hesitated but then pushed me up close and lifted my arm to the keyboard. My hand fell limp. My fingers couldn't begin to press the keys. I barely heard my family's consoling words – that I'd been very sick, that more physical therapy would improve my muscles, that rehabilitation takes time, etc. I do remember Mother leaving the room so that I wouldn't see her crying.

Reality began to hit me. I hadn't expected much of myself while at the hospital where, like all patients, I was sick, confined to a bed and attended by nurses. But now at home it was different. All the usual normal activities one takes for granted were visibly beyond my ability. I was no longer sick – no fever, no nausea, but I was living in a different body – one that didn't work.

The experience of being dependent on others for everything was humbling and frustrating, but there was nothing I could do about it.

Exhausted after the day's events, I was carried to bed. Being home was not what I had expected it to be. I felt out of place. How can one who is unable to take part in life feel "at home" when everyone else is buzzing about being busy with various normal activities? Going to Georgia began to seem less dreadful. Realizing to some degree what my parents had been going through, I felt the responsibility to ease their worries by putting forth a positive attitude about leaving.

Wendell returned the next morning with the ambulance to take me and my parents to the airport. The airline personnel were helpful in providing a place for me to lie down for the three-hour flight to Atlanta. From Atlanta, another ambulance ride took us seventy miles to our destination – the Georgia Warm Springs Foundation.

The rehabilitation facility was more like a beautiful college campus than a hospital, with white colonial-style buildings, winding walkways and pillared colonnades. The grounds had lots of fir trees and tall pines. Georgia Hall was the main building where we checked in. It had a huge lobby with ample room for patients and visitors to congregate. At one end, double doors opened up into the dining hall. It was a large, well-decorated room with tall windows that provided a lovely view of the landscape. Tables for four were set with white tablecloths and cloth napkins, and waiters served the food. Quite elegant for a hospital! There was a fleet of teenage push-boys in white uniforms whose job was to take the patients from place to place and building to building.

Although my parents hated to leave me at Warm Springs alone, once I was settled in and evaluated (a three day process), the doctors convinced them that I'd adjust better if they left. And I did.

Thus, I entered into a new period of learning, for so it was.

Chapter 5

I shared a room with a girl from West Virginia. There were several nurses' aides on our wing during the day to see to the needs of the patients, and to get us ready for our physical therapy. They were very kind and congenial, and I'm grateful for all they did for me. At night, however, there was only one nurse on duty. Most of the patients were either able to turn themselves or could sleep through the night without turning. Because I was still in the stage of severe muscle soreness, I needed to be turned often, and Miss Dawson hated being disturbed from whatever she was doing at the nurses' station. The nights seemed endless and I missed my mother's tender care.

I was fitted for a corset with steel staves and heavy straps that would enable me to sit upright and would protect my spine from developing a curvature. A wheelchair with arm-sling attachments and a lapboard was ordered for me. The leather arm-slings hung down from overhead metal bars and enabled me to move my arms by swinging them with just the slightest effort. With an open book placed on the lapboard, I learned that by swinging my arm, my fingers could drag across and turn the page. On my first trip to the brace shop, I was measured for metal hand-splints that kept my wrists straight and my fingers in a normal position.

Sarah Margaret Smith

Before being able to have my meals in the dining hall, I had to learn to feed myself. A special piece of equipment, called a feeder, was made for me. It was a small metal stand that could hook onto the edge of a table. A curved piece of metal that tilted up and down was attached to the top of the stand to cradle my forearm. With a spoon or fork secured onto my hand splint, I was able to bring bites of food up to my mouth. Once I was outfitted with all this paraphernalia, I felt something like the Tin Man in the *Wizard of Oz*, but I fit right in with the other patients.

Physical therapy began shortly after breakfast with a table treatment. The therapist would slowly move and bend my neck, my arms, legs, every finger and toe. She would grade the strength of each muscle – zero, trace, poor, fair, good or normal. In order to stimulate my back and shoulder muscles, she would first apply ice.

Next on the schedule was therapy in a large indoor pool. After being dressed in a swimsuit and covered with a blanket, a push boy would come to pick me up, put me onto a gurney and take me to the pool area. There the therapists would lift me onto one of the many tables that were submerged in the pool. Only the headrests were above water. The warm water from the natural mineral springs was relaxing. The buoyancy allowed my legs and arms to float and move slightly with the help of the therapist. Occasionally, a muscle that had appeared to be lifeless would suddenly contract. I gained a bit of strength each week from the treatments.

After the therapy I was taken into a dressing room where two attendants were to remove my bathing suit, dry me off, dress me in my pajamas, cover me with a blanket and send for a push boy to take me back to my room. These particular young women attendants were totally insensitive to a patient's feelings of modesty and enjoyed causing embarrassment. They would strip me naked and leave me shivering on the gurney in front of them while they sat down, drank a Coke and made remarks like, *"What's the matter, can't you take the cold?" "You're really a sissy, aren't you? What's the matter, don't you like being naked?"* Had I been older, I would have had the good sense to report their behavior but I was afraid of them. I told no one. However, someone evidently did report them for their rude behavior because they were soon fired from their job. The Warm Springs Foundation would not put up with that kind of behavior.

It seemed that I'd been stripped of everything – my physical strength, my family life, my social life, my privacy, and now, even my personal dignity. I certainly wasn't brave or strong. If anything, I was frail and timid and would have dissolved into tears if there had been anyone to turn to for consolation. I think we are quicker to fall apart emotionally when we know we have someone to cry with us. But when we have no one, we have no choice but to accept the situation and go on. That's what I did, and perhaps it was better that way.

I know now that as difficult as this may have been for me as a young girl, it was nothing compared to the indignation that my Blessed Savior Jesus endured. While my experience was less than a drop in the ocean by comparison, it has given me a better appreciation for all that He suffered on my behalf. He who was Righteous suffered for the unrighteous.

He was despised and rejected of men,

a man of sorrows and acquainted with grief...

He was oppressed, yet when he was afflicted

He opened not his mouth;

as a lamb that is led to the slaughter, and as

a sheep that before its shearers is dumb,

so He opened not his mouth.

Isaiah 53: 3, 7 ASV

After lunch and a long rest, I had an hour of occupational therapy. There I began to learn to do practical things like feeding myself, combing my hair, writing with my left hand, etc. I was naturally right-handed but my right hand was showing no signs of improvement, so I was learning to use my left hand for everything.

After two weeks, I was over my soreness and was moved to a four-bed ward. My roommates were Betty from Alabama, Marcia from Michigan and Leona from New Mexico. They each had been there for months and "knew the ropes." They were very helpful to me. Not only for my sake, but also for their own, they devised a plan that would do away with my need for enemas. Every evening Nurse Dawson would come by and offer one laxative pill to anyone needing it. The dosage was not working for me, so I was subjected to the embarrassment of an enema every other

In the Shadow of His Hand

day. Therefore, the girls decided to request pills for themselves, even though they didn't need them, and give them to me to take. To say the least, that one mega-dose did the trick and set me on the Road to Regularity!

Leona was a character who instigated lots of mischief. For her birthday she had her brother bring a live horned toad, a ghastly-looking critter, in a gift-wrapped box. She purposely opened it in front of Miss Dawson, scaring the poor woman out of her wits!

There were lots of young people my age at the Foundation, and we all became friends. Some were severely handicapped and some less handicapped, but what we shared in common enabled us to overlook the physical and to appreciate each other for who we really were. We laughed and joked together like young people do and seldom discussed our physical problems. We spent enough time with the therapists everyday, talking about those things. The atmosphere was something like being at camp, although the lessons we were learning were far different from learning to row a boat or build a camp fire.

The push-boys brought a bit of levity to the daily routine. They'd jump on the back of our wheelchairs while taking us down a sloping walkway and we'd coast along, laughing all the way to the bottom of the hill. Sometimes they'd sit in wheelchairs and race along doing wheelies. One Sunday, a busload of tourists arrived to tour the famous Warm Springs Foundation, having heard of the therapeutic waters. Several of us, including one of the push boys who was sitting in a wheelchair, had gathered around near the fountain outside of Georgia Hall. As the people walked by staring at us, the push boy suddenly and purposely fell over out of the wheelchair and into the fountain. He jumped up, soaking wet with his arms in the air, yelling, *"I'm healed,*

I'm healed!" I don't think the tourists appreciated his prank, but we got a kick out of it.

Sitting with friends at Warm Springs

Once a week we had Movie Night. A big barn on the grounds had been converted into a movie theater for the patients. About eighty of us, some in wheelchairs, some on crutches, some on gurneys, would attend this weekly event. The wood frame barn was old and the local fire department always sent their truck to park right outside whenever a movie was shown. I'll never forget one night after I had been at Warm Springs several months, when we saw the movie *"The Men,"* with Marlon Brando. Some may have thought this an inappropriate movie for a group of handicapped people to watch, thinking it might be discouraging. However, we found it quite humorous. This melodramatic depiction of a wounded soldier who became paralyzed from the waist down was nothing short of laughable to us "polio veterans." Not that we were insensitive to his physical condition, it was his attitude and self-pity that were absurd to us. However, I wonder how good our attitudes would have been had we not been at Warm Springs. Although separated from the real world, we learned lessons just from being there that helped us to have a sensible perspective and prepared us for life back home.

After Christmas, teachers from the local high school began coming to give private schooling. I still ended up a half year behind my class, but my parents let me fly home in May for a few days to attend their graduation. Mother planned a patio party for the class with Mexican food and a Mariachi band. The kids brought and signed each other's senior yearbooks. I was surprised to see a page dedicated to me from the class, even though I wasn't graduating with them.

I enjoyed seeing my friends again. They laughed and danced and had a great time at the party. They talked about where they were planning to go to college, and what sorority or fraternity they were going to pledge. I was glad for them, but college had never interested me much. The drudgery of four more years of school was not the way I wanted to spend my time. More education didn't seem all that important to me. Neither of my parents had gone much beyond elementary school and yet they were well-educated in most things important for life and happiness. They were intelligent and had lots of good common sense. They kept

Sarah Margaret Smith

up with the times and were involved in political and civic affairs. My dad, proud to be an American citizen but never forgetting his humble roots, served on the Dallas Council on World Affairs during the 1950s and early 60s. My parents' lack of formal education didn't hinder or bother them at all, and they were at ease in any social setting.

My heart's desire had always been to marry and have a family, but at this point I wondered if it could ever happen. Again, I was faced with the fact that my life was different because of polio. Most of my friends were great and I enjoyed being with them, but there were those who were uncomfortable around me, not knowing what to say. In some ways I felt too old to be a part of the group anymore, and in other ways I felt too young.

It was good to get back to Warm Springs. With a long metal brace on my right leg, I began learning to walk. Crutches were strapped to my arms and I moved them one at a time as I hunched my shoulders, right then left, and slowly took steps. My shoulders would soon tire out, and I found myself dragging the crutches along as I walked. I begged the therapist to let me try walking without them but she wouldn't allow it. My hopes were high that eventually I would be able to walk without the brace or the crutches. I could feel my legs getting stronger. I knew that my right arm probably would never improve but I was learning to use my left arm and hand. My handwriting was actually becoming legible, and I was allowed, at last, to dispense with wearing the arm slings and hand splints.

At my final "clinic," a monthly meeting where patients met with the doctors and therapists for their evaluation, I was disheartened to hear their comments. Dr. Bernard ended the discussion by speaking into a recorder. *"Patient is being discharged on October 20, after eleven months of therapy here at the Foundation. She will be permanently wheelchair-bound. She has been equipped with crutches and a long-leg brace on her right leg, but her arms are too weak to use the crutches properly or beneficially. Therefore, walking will never be practical for her. Once lifted to her feet, she is able to stand and turn with help in order to transfer from bed to chair, etc., but taking more than a few steps without her leg brace will eventually cause severe hyperextension of the knee. This would necessitate surgery to stabilize the knee joint. Such surgery would prevent her from bending the knee. She must continue wearing a corset or else scoliosis will increase, thus limiting her ability to sit comfortably."*

I couldn't imagine going through life with my right leg sticking straight out whenever I sat, so I knew I would have to wear my leg brace. But I resented the doctor's overall evaluation and couldn't believe he could be so certain that my condition wasn't going to improve. Nonetheless, his report put a damper on my hopes. Up to that time the attitude at Warm Springs had been positive and encouraging. *"Come on, you can do it!"* *"Keep it up, you're getting better!"* Apparently, I had had too much muscle loss, and they were discharging me because no more improvement was expected.

Chapter 6

My parents and my brother Arge drove out to Georgia to take me back to Dallas. I did a lot of thinking, as well as some secret crying, on that trip. I was going to miss the camaraderie among the patients at Warm Springs. We had learned and shared so much together. Our experiences there had taught us something about hard struggles, small successes and disappointing failures. We rejoiced over the tiniest accomplishments, whether it was buttoning a button or writing our names. I'd learned I could often substitute a normal method with an innovation, like using my teeth instead of my hand to open tubes of lipstick or toothpaste. I found I could paint with a paintbrush in my mouth. Such substitutions gave me no embarrassment in front of other patients, but how would it be in front of the able-bodied? They'd surely consider me peculiar, or look on me with pity, and I dreaded that. The closer we got to Dallas the more I realized I wanted to look "normal." But I found I was selling most people short. Of course, there were stares from strangers and pitying looks, even from people I knew, but my closest friends were still my closest friends. Even though we were not bonded by a crippling disease, we had shared much over the years, and our friendships were based on more than just one common experience.

Friendships made at Warm Springs were important for the time, but just for that time. The unspoken fact was that once we left the confines of the Foundation we would go our separate ways back to our real lives. Our experience at Warm Springs and those friendships would all be put away in the past. Although we exchanged addresses, promising to write, we soon lost touch with one another.

Somehow, like most little girls, I had grown up expecting my life to be like a fairytale, and that the good things I wanted for myself would surely come true. Now, I began to understand that there would be unusual challenges ahead of me. I had met patients who were physically much worse off, and some who had little or no emotional support from family. They'd be going home to face harder adjustments than those I would encounter. Having seen so many with similar or worse physical problems than my own helped me to accept and not bemoan my situation.

Whether or not I improved, I knew I would have to tough it out. I owed it to my parents. Growing up in a time and in a family in which one was expected to face difficulties with grit and determination, I didn't want to let anyone down, not even myself. Both my parents had great fortitude, and I had seen them get through difficult situations without crumbling. My father exhibited a Greek stoicism, and my mother, also, showed great strength and resilience in the face of trials.

While at Warm Springs, I had talked with patients who came back for checkups. It was encouraging to see that they were able to embrace life by pursuing their studies or finding employment in spite of their disabilities. Some had married and were looking forward to having children. I began to see that a physical disability didn't have to be a detriment to living a good life.

During those first few weeks back home, I continued my exercises with a physical therapist that came to the house three times a week. I did a lot of reading and enjoyed being around my family. I went through a short period of homesickness for Warm Springs, missing that comfortable environment where being handicapped was normal. My mother was very perceptive and could sense when I was feeling down. She would talk to me and let me cry on her shoulder. After I cried it out, my spirits would lift and I would wonder why I had been sad. I didn't really want to be back at Warm Springs, but adjusting to life at home was emotionally taxing at times.

My dad was such a positive person and was always coming up with ideas to strengthen my muscles. He paid no attention to the doctor's final analysis of my condition. Soon after I got home from Warm Springs, he had an enclosed heated swimming pool built in our backyard and insisted that I go in the water at least five times a week. It was complete with parallel bars for me to walk between and a lift to put me in and out of the water. This was the very best therapy I could have had. I began to have better balance and more endurance. I quit wearing the corset. Not only was it extremely uncomfortable, it seemed to hinder rather than help my walking. Soon, I was more and more tempted to take a few steps without my leg brace and simply held someone's hand for security. Remembering Dr. Bernard's warnings, however, kept me from overdoing it. The brace was cumbersome, but Mother would put it on me daily, and I would practice walking from one end of the house to the other, hunching along with my crutches.

I soon got used to being at home, and the longing for Warm Springs left.

Within the human spirit there seems to be a marvelous defense mechanism that, when utilized, protects

In the Shadow of His Hand

us from being dragged down emotionally. Whenever I thought of pleasurable things I could no longer do, I would dismiss those thoughts before they brought on sadness. For example, I could talk about having studied and played the piano, but I couldn't let myself dwell on how much I missed it. I don't think it was because I was such a strong person. Maybe it was because I wasn't strong enough to reflect on such things very long without becoming depressed. Who knows? All I know is that I simply hated the feeling of sadness. I found it dreary and miserable, so, with this survival tactic, the sad thoughts were quickly blocked from taking over my mind and emotions.

Psychologists would probably call this a form of denial, but for me it was healthy. They would want to open up all these feelings and examine them until they became overblown and, dare I suggest, even idolized. (I say this because a few years later at a rehabilitation center in California where I spent a few months, I was obligated to have one session with a psychologist before being dismissed from that program. He seemed very intent on proving to me that I was unhappy.)

Eager to get on with my life, I went back to high school for one semester and graduated in January 1952. Chris made me a beautiful white graduation dress, and one of my classmates pushed me across the stage to receive my diploma. I settled into a simple routine at home and began taking private Greek lessons. Mr. Foster, my teacher, came to the house three times a week for two-hour lessons.

That summer, my brother Arge married. He and his 17-year-old bride moved in with us for a while until they could find a place of their own. Pauline and I spent a lot of time together while my brother was at work. She hadn't learned to drive so we were stuck at home day after day until I had a brainstorm. I would teach her how to drive!

Sarah Margaret Smith

Knowing that my brother would never permit such a dangerous escapade, I persuaded Pauline to keep it a secret from him. Oddly enough, I even convinced my mother to let us use her car. Fearless and with all confidence, we began our clandestine pursuit. In order to keep Pauline from going too fast, I scooted over next to her and had her place my left foot under the gas pedal so that she could push it down only so far. Actually, this worked out fairly well as we went very slowly around the block several times. The next day we were at it again bright and early. As we approached the corner of the block a little too fast, I said, *"Turn quick, Pauline,"* and she plowed right into a group of wooden mailboxes, knocking them over. Shaken and scared of being found out, we inched our way home and asked Bill, our longtime yard man who had often helped me out of bad scrapes, to go repair the damage, swearing him to secrecy. We were undaunted by this mishap, and by the next week we were ready to venture down to the neighborhood shopping center. As we were driving along in the traffic, a man began backing his car out of a parking place. For fear he didn't see us, I shouted, *"Honk, Pauline!"* But instead of honking, Pauline slammed on the brakes so hard that I fell down onto the floorboard. Traffic behind us stopped as Pauline jumped out of the car and came around to pull me up onto the seat. Although our cars had not collided, the man, feeling somewhat responsible, got out of his car to see what had happened to me. Seeing my inability to help myself up, he was greatly distressed and said, *"Shouldn't we call an ambulance? She's been injured!"* *"Oh, no. She's fine,"* Pauline answered as she jumped back in the car and drove off, leaving the man standing there completely perplexed.

Chapter 7

Still a close observer of life around me, I watched my brothers and sisters establish their own homes, adjust to married life and raise their little ones. They would congregate at our home often and keep us up on the daily events of their lives, the joys as well as the trials. It seemed that sooner or later every predicament and every crisis would be brought home, usually just to Mama. My dad, being more austere and outspoken with his advice, would be approached with a bit of trepidation. Although my parents may have laid a heavy burden on their married children by being so closely involved in their lives, right or wrong, their motivation was purely out of love. I could see this, perhaps better than my siblings, because I lived at home and heard my parents express their loving concern for each of their children.

School friends would call or come by from time to time. A boy that had liked me since junior high school told a buddy of his, *"I would marry Margaret in a minute if she hadn't had polio."* His friend, thinking this was a grand compliment, told me what Joe had said! For a few days I felt hurt. Not that I wanted to marry Joe, but I sank into a slump of thinking that no one could ever love me. Then I remembered something my father had told me. Ironically, only a few months before I got sick, he had advised me not to consider teenage crushes to be real love. He said that if I happened to be disfigured in a car accident, a boy with merely a teenage crush on me wouldn't hang around for very long; but when a man really loves a woman, he loves her no matter what happens. My dad's words echoed in my mind and gave me a measure of hope. I knew I was much better off without Joe's teenage kind of love.

Soon after that, a local priest paid us a pastoral visit. As we sat talking, the conversation turned to me and my physical condition – how I was doing, etc. The priest commented that he knew a nice young woman in the Ohio town where he grew up who had been paralyzed from polio. I assumed he was about to give me some encouragement, but he went on to say in words dripping with somber pity, *"She is in really bad shape like you are, Margaret. And I can hardly believe it but I hear she's actually been dating a man, and he has asked her to marry him! I just can't imagine why he would marry her."* I was somewhat taken aback at his comment and I replied tersely, *"Well, maybe he loves her!"* It was strange that thoughtless and insensitive words came from the most unexpected sources.

Again I reflected on what my father had told me about true love, and I refused to be discouraged. It was becoming obvious to me that there are people who are incapable of seeing beyond the physical, and that they themselves suffer from a worse handicap, a mental one. Perhaps they are the ones who should be pitied.

Being around my siblings was a great emotional tonic for me. They made me feel that I was a part of their lives, taking me places with them and having me over to spend the night. There was no attitude of pity; rather, my physical disabilities were accepted and looked on merely as a slight inconvenience. Inevitably, these inconveniences would put me into a comical situation that kept us laughing.

There was no benefit in feeling self-conscious, even though certain situations could be frustrating and even embarrassing at times. When I was invited to go out with friends who were not used to taking care of me, I would get nervous, almost making myself sick. I finally learned not to take myself or my struggles so seriously. Seeing the humor in a predicament made it easier for me, and set others at ease, as well.

Still skinny as a bean pole, it was difficult to find clothes that would fit. Once, my mother and I were shopping at a neighborhood dress shop. Mother helped me to my feet and held on to me while the nice sales lady dressed me. After trying a number of dresses that swallowed me, she brought in a two-piece outfit. The blouse fit okay and, determined to make a sale, she threw the skirt over my head, buttoned it and exclaimed excitedly, *"It's a perfect fit!"* The only problem was she had forgotten that my arms were still hanging at my sides inside the skirt, taking up the slack. Mother and I cracked up laughing as we looked in the full-length mirror. The sales lady, still unaware of what she had done, was ready to write out a sales ticket. *"It does seem to fit well,"* mother commented dryly, *"but what about her arms?"*

The next purchase my dad made was an electric stationary bicycle which he set up in my room. This, I hated. Actually, it was a bit too rigorous for me even on the lowest speed. He would help me on it, and Mother would strap my hands to the handlebars. I tried it for a few weeks then gave it up.

Even though I was getting stronger, a head cold would put me in bed for a week or two with chills and fever. The doctor would come to the house to check me over.

43

There was always the danger of pneumonia because of my weak lung capacity and my inability to cough normally.

I returned to Warm Springs the summer of 1953 for surgery on my left hand. By the rerouting of a flexor muscle from my finger to my thumb, I was enabled to grip and pick up things more easily. This greatly improved my handwriting, as well.

***

Since taking care of me was becoming too much for my mom who suffered with a bad hip, she and Daddy decided to hire a live-in helper for me. This turned into quite an adventure! The first several applicants were totally unacceptable. Then, in desperation we hired a woman who looked like she could have been a prison guard. She lasted two weeks. I didn't like having a "keeper," especially someone like Mrs. Brumhalter. We tried several others, but not one was right for the job. My dad then decided to apply for a displaced person from Europe. A young Greek woman in her early twenties named Dora arrived, and we were all excited to welcome her into our family. The only problem was she wasn't a bit happy about coming to America to live with us. We did all we could to make her feel comfortable. We even took her with us to the Greek AHEPA convention in New York City. She was obviously delighted to see all the Greek people in the hotel lobby. While my parents would be busy with meetings and social obligations, Dora was told to stay with me and help with whatever I needed. But the first afternoon she disappeared. My dad called Hotel Security and the search began. She was discovered in the hotel bar trying to make dates with men. It turned out that Dora was a prostitute. My dad was furious with her. He had taken her into our family and tried to be like a father to her.

In the Shadow of His Hand

He marched her up to the hotel room she and I shared. While he was questioning her, she smarted off at him, cursing at him, and he slapped her. I was as surprised as she was, but relieved that it hadn't been a hard slap at all, nor did it leave even a mark on her face. Dora was indignant and charged out of the room, down the hall and onto the elevator. In a few minutes, two men from hotel security knocked at the door. They explained that Dora was accusing my dad of physical abuse and they wanted to question me alone. Although I felt I was in a court of law and knew I was supposed to tell the truth, I lied when they asked me if my father had slapped Dora. Deep down inside, I knew it was a sin to bear false witness, but I couldn't bring myself to testify against my dad. I loved him too much and I knew he had not hurt the girl. This sin was a bit harder for me to justify than any other sin I had ever committed, and it bothered me for some time. As soon as we got back to Dallas, Daddy shipped Dora off to her cousin in Illinois.

The next girl sent to us was a German refugee who had fled Nazi Germany with her family. We all enjoyed Gretchen. She knew very little English but wanted to learn, and I was interested in learning German from her. So, with a Berlitz book and a dictionary, we taught each other. She stayed with us for almost two years.

My dad was concerned about my having something to do with my life. He wanted me to have a career, and at one point he tried to set me up in business. The sister of a business acquaintance of his was a fashion designer who wanted to design and sell formal evening dresses to department stores and boutiques, but she lacked the money to get started. Although I enjoyed art and was beginning to be able to draw a little with my left hand, I wasn't very good and had no experience in dress design or commercial art in any form. Daddy said I would learn and that I could surely

45

Sarah Margaret Smith

do it! He was willing to put up the money for my share of the business, but before the papers were signed, he investigated the woman's financial situation and found her to be deeply in debt. Actually, I was relieved when he canceled the deal.

Then one day he brought home a small machine that would emboss initials or designs on stationery. All one had to do was insert the paper and press down the lever. It proved to be much too strenuous for me.

When some of my nieces and nephews began showing an interest in music, their parents asked me to teach them piano. I went back to Miss Schawe, my piano teacher, to get some pointers on teaching. All those years I had studied were now to be used in a very special way in my life. I enjoyed teaching the children, and soon some of their friends and several neighborhood children began taking lessons. Before long I was teaching every afternoon for two or three hours. At last, I had a vocation that I could do and that I loved.

By then my sister Alethia began urging me to take some courses at SMU. I had no idea what I wanted to study. I enjoyed writing, so I decided to take English. At that time, the buildings were not handicap-accessible. Not knowing any of the students, it was difficult finding young men who would volunteer to carry me up the long flights of stairs. I quit after one semester. I decided to take French at the Berlitz School of Language and continued my private Greek lessons at home with Mr. Foster.

Alethia, being an artist, also helped me get started with oil painting. It was slow and messy but I enjoyed it. Going into the pool daily, teaching piano, studying Greek and French and piddling with art kept me fairly busy.

My social life consisted of going with my parents to parties given by family friends, attending church and church

46

In the Shadow of His Hand

functions and singing in the church choir. A few close girlfriends were good about taking me with them to dinner or to the movies. They didn't seem to mind the ordeal of getting me in and out of the car and into my portable wheelchair. We would find ourselves often in funny predicaments. For example, one Saturday afternoon I went with two of my girlfriends to the Majestic Theater to see "Gone with the Wind." They took two seats at the end of a row and parked me in my wheelchair right next to them in the aisle. During the dramatic scene in which Atlanta was burning, two elderly women and an even older man came down the steep aisle looking for a place to sit. The theater was packed, but the two women noticed three empty seats further down on our row. They carefully stepped around the front of my foot pedals and made their way down the row, motioning to the old man to follow. However, instead of stepping around my pedals, the man stepped *on* my pedals. This tilted the chair forward, causing my knees to hit him behind his knees, which caused him to sit down in my lap! On impulse I said, *"Sir, this seat is taken!"* With his feet still on my foot pedals, he jumped up. Once again my chair tilted forward, my knees hit him behind his knees and he plopped down in my lap. With this, the brakes on my chair unlocked and we began to roll down the aisle together. My friend quickly grabbed onto the chair and pulled it back before we went very far. For a moment there I imagined us landing in the orchestra pit! With my friend's help, the man finally got his feet planted on the floor but refused to try stepping over me. Instead, he chose to make his way down the row behind us. When he reached his women friends, he climbed over the seat and sat down!

Chapter 8

My dad had promised me a trip to Greece to meet my relatives there, once I learned the language. Of course, I couldn't go alone, so Daddy paid for Sue Greenly, who was working for us at the time, to go with me. Two of my girlfriends, Lily and Harriet, were planning a trip that summer, and we arranged to meet in various places throughout Europe before ending up in Greece. It was quite an adventure and a wonderful three month vacation.

Air travel back then was a dress up affair. I carefully picked out a tailored dress with matching jacket, white shoes, and a hat with a short veil. Because our luggage weight was limited, we each bought the largest purses we could find and stuffed them with cosmetics, shoes, film, and various sundries we considered necessary. Loaded down with cameras, purses, and my leg brace slung over Sue's shoulder, we began our trip as excited as Cornelia Otis Skinner and Emily Kimbrough, authors of the hilarious book about their travels, *Our Hearts Were Young and Gay*. (Of course, back then the word *gay* meant *merry* or *lighthearted*).

I had to be carried up the steps of the plane because there were no jet-ways out to the aircraft in 1959. The airlines had notified each airport that I would need

In the Shadow of His Hand

assistance upon my arrival in their city. Our first stop was in London. After the other passengers deplaned, two very polite but scrawny little men came to carry me down the steps. Neither felt competent on his own to carry me, so with one man on my right side and one man on my left, they hoisted me up, each grabbing a leg and an arm. They carried me down the narrow stairway and plopped me into my wheelchair which had been retrieved from the baggage compartment. By this time my hat was askew and one shoe had fallen off. Sue was running along behind, carrying all the stuff. From there, they wheeled me over to an awaiting ambulance, of all things, lifted me up once again in their arms and laid me down on a stretcher. Then, the ambulance took us about a hundred yards to the airport terminal.

In Stockholm, after being carried down to my wheelchair, I was lifted, wheelchair and all, into the back of a pickup truck. Each airport throughout Europe was a unique experience.

My arrival in Athens was memorable and quite touching. One of my uncles lived in Elevsina, a suburb of Athens, and the other lived in the village of Melissi where my father was born. Both uncles and their families came to the airport to welcome me with bouquets of flowers and lots of hugs, kisses and happy tears. Sue and I spent two weeks sightseeing in Athens, with Uncle Haralambos as our tour guide. Visiting the Acropolis was no easy task. The taxi driver lifted me up in his arms and carried me all the way while my uncle dragged the wheelchair along. Making several rest stops, we finally reached the top of the hill. I was grateful for the opportunity to see the ancient ruins that had stood there for centuries. It was an incredible sight.

Up to the Acropolis

Eager to visit with more of the relatives and to see my father's birthplace, we left Athens and traveled by taxi to Melissi which overlooked the Corinthian Gulf. Since the bathroom facilities at the homes of my relatives were not adequate for me (no indoor plumbing), we checked into a small hotel in the neighboring town of Xylokastron. My uncle made arrangements with a taxi driver to take us to the village the next day. Our driver Stavros was very proud of his ten-year-old American-made Chevrolet that he had equipped with outside speakers. We sped along the narrow

In the Shadow of His Hand

winding highway with Greek music blasting away. When we entered the village, people came out of their homes waving and shouting, *"The American girl! The American girl!"* Evidently, the news that I was coming to visit had spread throughout the village and they were all waiting to welcome me.

After a huge late lunch, we all bedded down for an afternoon rest, as is the Greek custom. I was amazed that shops closed and even radio stations went off the air for several hours. The evening meal was generally served after nine o'clock.

Uncle Spiro was aghast that my parents would allow me to travel so far away from home, especially in my physical condition. Therefore, he felt a grave responsibility to watch over me, even though I was twenty-five years old.

We soon learned that news inevitably would spread like wildfire from Xylokastron to Melissi. One day Sue and I went to the beach instead of taking a rest. That evening when we went to Melissi to have dinner with the relatives, Uncle Spiro already knew about our being at the beach all afternoon and that we hadn't even worn hats to protect our faces from the sun!

Every day was a new adventure. Uncle Spiro didn't have a car, but he did have a motorcycle with a trailer hitched to the back of it. We would all pile in it for a bumpy ride up to the grape vineyards or to a neighboring town to visit other relatives.

When Sue and I decided to rent a car for one day and drive to Olympia to meet up with my friends Lily and Harriet, my uncle was totally against it. He had absolutely no confidence in Sue's driving ability and was certain that we would have an accident. I assured him he had nothing to worry about. We left early the next morning, met my friends in Olympia, did some sight-seeing and had a late lunch together. Driving back that afternoon, just before we got to Xylokastron, a bee flew into the car and landed on my arm. I screamed, *"There's a bee on me!"* When Sue tried to shoo it out the window, the car careened off the road, crashed through a fence and hit a tree in the middle of a lemon orchard. I landed on the floorboard of the car with leaves and broken glass from the window in my hair. Sue suffered only a minor bump on the head. After realizing we were okay, my next thought was, *"Oh, no. I hope Uncle Spiro doesn't find out about this!"* Then the owner of the property came running, yelling that we had ruined his fence and broken branches off three of his lemon trees. I promised to pay for the damage. Needless to say, the news reached Melissi before we did.

The people of Greece have a beautiful way of showing hospitality. I was overwhelmed by their generosity. They had opened up their hearts and their homes to show their love. My cousin Sophia and I had become close friends, and I hated to leave, but after almost three months in Greece, we said our tearful goodbyes.

We flew on to Rome for a short stay, and then to Barcelona, Spain. As in most European cities, many of the taxis had the rear passenger seat far back from the car door. One would have to step up into the cab first in order to sit down. Since that was beyond my capabilities, we always had to check to see if a taxi would be accessible for me. One day after shopping in a department store on a busy street in Barcelona, we looked for a taxi to take us back to our hotel. The first one that came along stopped; the driver jumped out and opened the door for us, but we saw immediately that it was the wrong kind of taxi. We apologized and tried to explain to the driver why we couldn't take his cab, but he was furious! He actually wanted us to pay him for stopping. Evidently, he had already started the meter running before

In the Shadow of His Hand

he opened the door for us. Of course, we refused to pay and quickly went our way down the block, leaving him shouting that he would have us arrested. In a few minutes we looked back and saw him walking briskly in our direction accompanied by a police officer. We quickly turned the corner, darted undetected into a dress shop and exited through a back door, evading arrest!

Throughout the trip I was often finding myself in places where the doorways were too narrow for my wheelchair, and I would have to get up and walk a few steps. Elevators caused a different problem. Many of them had two sets of double doors – the outer doors would swing out and the inner doors would swing in. Maneuvering a wheelchair in and out wasn't easy. As all this proved to be a constant inconvenience, I gradually began walking more and using my wheelchair less.

Our last stop was in Madrid, where I bought a new dress, new shoes with one and a half inch heals (such a thrill after having to wear flat heals for so long) and visited a swanky beauty salon where I got a new hairdo! By the time we got back to Dallas, I was seldom using the wheelchair except for long distances.

Arriving at Love Field, I walked to the door of the plane after all the other passengers had exited and stood there waiting for my brother to come carry me down the steps. My dad rushed up the steps first, looked at me and didn't recognize me! *"Daddy, it's me,"* I said. Everyone was astonished at my improvement.

***

I was thrilled with the new feeling of independence after nine years of being wheelchair-bound. I still required assistance to get up out of a chair, but once I was up I felt almost normal. The leg brace we had needlessly wagged about with us all over Europe was thrown into a closet, along with the crutches, never to be used again! I thought to myself, *"If only that doctor at Warm Springs could see me now!"*

With new optimism, I began to envision one day being strong enough to take care of myself. I imagined even falling in love and getting married, if ever the right one came along who loved me with that true kind of love my dad had spoken about.

Thinking I might need to be checked over by a doctor, my parents made an appointment for me with an orthopedist in Dallas, one I'd never seen, who worked with polio patients. After a complete muscle test by the physical therapist, a nurse helped me dress, and then ushered me into the doctor's office. He was sitting at his desk looking at the results of my muscle test. *"Well, Margaret,"* he said, *"I must tell you that by looking at these test results, I would never have expected you to walk in here on your own as you just did. Even though your glutes are fair, you have little more than a trace of quadriceps, hamstrings, hip flexors, adductors, or abductors. Your back, shoulder and stomach muscles are extremely weak. Polio hit you hard from the neck down, didn't it? Remarkably, it seems that you regained a muscle here and a muscle there, in strategic places throughout your body that are enough, just barely enough, to enable you to walk. It's absolutely amazing! Somehow they all work together in spite of how the test results look on paper."*

In the Shadow of His Hand

I will praise Thee;
for I am fearfully and wonderfully made:
Marvelous are Thy works;
and that my soul knoweth right well.

Psalm 139:14

Chapter 9

I spent the next few months trying to learn to dress and bathe myself. I was tired of having a live-in helper always around. My mom said, *"But won't you miss having someone to help you and drive you places?"* I tried to explain to her that being able to take care of myself, even though it wasn't easy, did more for me than having a nursemaid and running around with her as my chauffeur. I learned to get in and out of bed by myself, and with the use of various gadgets, some I'd seen advertised in medical catalogs and some I invented, I eventually reached my goal of taking care of my personal needs.

By putting a thick firm cushion in a straight chair, I discovered I was able to get up by myself. What freedom it was to walk about in the house, to sit, and to get up whenever I wanted, without having to bother someone to help me! It was exciting learning to do things on my own, and I was overjoyed with even the smallest physical achievements. With this measure of independence, I was optimistic about my life and no longer concerned about being different. I felt very fortunate that with polio, unlike multiple sclerosis or muscular dystrophy, patients continue to get better over time, not worse – or so I thought.

In the Shadow of His Hand

With all my jubilation, however, I must confess I never truly thanked the Lord for the wonderful improvement. I was excited about it and I felt fortunate but seldom considered where the good fortune came from. Oh, I would say things like, *"Thank God I can get around better now,"* in a casual sense, instead of bowing my head in humble gratitude to the Lord who is *"the healer of all our diseases."* Instead of desiring to live my life to His honor and glory, I became preoccupied with enjoying my "almost normal" life. No longer self-conscious about my disability, I was eager to go places and meet people.

But walking, I soon found out, had its dangers. Many times I would lose my balance or trip, crashing to the floor and have to be taken to emergency to be stitched up. Having a measure of independence definitely had its price, but it was worth every bruise.

Two years later, my parents and I made a trip to Greece together. My cousin Sophia was getting married and asked us to come for the wedding. She was only eighteen and her fiancé was a man she barely knew. As was the custom, the parents had arranged the prospective marriage. Once they were engaged, he was allowed to come over every Sunday evening to visit Sophia. They would sit on the patio in two straight chairs for their rendezvous while my uncle and aunt watched from the window. When I asked Sophia if she loved him, she said, *"No, not yet."* Then I asked how she knew that she *would* love him. She replied, *"I will love him because he will be my husband!"* At the time, I thought this to be ludicrous but, I must admit, her commitment was admirable.

It proved to be a happy marriage, in spite of a rocky start. After returning from their honeymoon, Sophia suffered some sort of emotional upset and was taken to a psychiatric hospital in Athens not far from our hotel. My dad received a frantic phone call from the bridegroom's brother, a schoolteacher. *"This is the Teacher,"* he yelled. Unused to using the telephone, many of the villagers, including the highly esteemed teacher, thought you had to yell into the telephone. *"Who?"* my dad asked. *"The Teacher! The Teacher! Come quick! Sophia is out of her mind!"* As we drove up to the hospital, we saw a nurse with a hypodermic needle chasing poor Sophia around the parking lot. My dad quickly intervened, grabbed Sophia's arm, led her to the taxi and dismissed the nurse. We took her to the hotel with us where she rested a few days and recovered. Apparently, she had been under much stress. Some of her in-laws had been unkind to her and Sophia just couldn't take it. They concluded that she was emotionally unstable and from bad stock. I found out later that they pointed out my physical condition as proof of genetic deficiencies in our family. On top of that, there were those who believed that because of my physical disabilities, I had put a demonic hex on Sophia. I was appalled at all the superstition.

The next year another trip to Greece was planned. This time my niece Maria, now age fourteen, would go with me. However, one week before we were to leave, I fell and broke my right arm. Maria and I both were disappointed, assuming the trip would have to be canceled. But the orthopedist surprised me by saying that my arm would not need to be put in a cast. He explained that because the break was near my shoulder and since I had no movement in my right arm, it really didn't need to be immobilized. He saw no reason why I should cancel our trip! His only advice was to be careful, wear a sling for a week or two and to take aspirin for the pain. So, off we went to Europe, broken arm and all.

Chris was a little apprehensive about Maria going with me to Greece and kept telling me, *"Be careful, and don't let my daughter drown in the Corinthian Gulf!"*

In the Shadow of His Hand

Watching over a cute little fourteen year old was a new experience for me. I had to rebuke one of the young hotel employees for getting too flirtatious with her.

We took a train trip from Xylokastron to the small city of Tripolis, and from there we taxied to the small village of Bitina to meet Maria's relatives on her mother's side. My cousin Giorgos came along to assist us. The train was jammed with passengers, and for the first thirty bumpy miles, we had to sit on our suitcases in the aisle. Many people brought their lunches and the smell of pork souvlaki and fried fish permeated the air. An old toothless woman dressed all in black sat near us holding a basket filled with pieces of watermelon. When she heard me speaking English to Maria, she frowned suspiciously and asked, *"Is she a foreigner?" "Yes, she is,"* I replied. *"You mean she's from Athens,"* she surmised. *"No,"* I explained, *"she's from America."* After staring at us for a few minutes, she offered to share her melon but, seeing the flies buzzing around it, we politely refused. With the motion of the train, the heat and the smell of the fish, I was surprised I made it to Tripolis without getting sick. We passed beautiful olive groves as the train wound its way through the mountainous region of the Peloponnesian peninsula. The higher altitude was cool and refreshing and the view from our hotel was breathtaking. The next day we drove to Bitina, a most primitive village. Children ran out to the road, excited to see an automobile. Some lived in houses with dirt floors. We located two of Maria's cousins and visited with them a few hours before returning to Xylokastron.

The remainder of our time in Greece we spent visiting with my relatives in and around Melissi. Sophia, now the mother of a three-week old little girl, was not allowed to leave her house for forty days. Anyone else entering or leaving the house would have to do so before midnight. This restriction was a tradition that was held to because of their fear of the "evil eye" that might come upon the mother or the newborn child.

Chapter 10

I continued teaching piano to children for the next few years, and while I enjoyed it, I wanted to do something that would take me out of the house – a job where I could meet people, some grown-up people. I was 28 years old. Most of my friends were married and having children. My parents were getting older and I knew I needed to learn how to live independently. I thought of getting an apartment in Dallas and looking for a job, but there was no way my family would allow me to live by myself, so I dismissed the idea. As a diversion, my friend Ruthie and I decided to join a Spanish class that met once a week in the evening. It was fun meeting new people. Occasionally, we would all go out to eat after the class. There was one man in particular who was especially nice and fun to talk with. I almost panicked when it became obvious that he was attracted to me. My physical disabilities didn't seem to bother him. He would help me up from a chair and in and out of the car as if it were a natural thing to do. This, of course, set me at ease and I was able to enjoy our time together. He asked me out and we dated for a while.

Around that time, Beth, a "polio" friend of mine who had moved to Houston, was working there as a speech therapist at the medical center. Her department needed someone to illustrate a booklet to be used as a teaching aid. Beth sent me the job which I did with some help from my sister. This opened up the idea for me to move to Houston. Oddly enough, it seemed it would be easier for my parents to accept my moving out of town because of a job, rather than into an apartment to live alone in Dallas for no apparent reason.

It took a lot of planning and thinking. My dad had always wanted me to be independent, but now that he was getting older and in poor health, he was beginning to rely on my being around all the time. I knew I had to move out while I could, before he got any sicker and more dependent on me. At the same time, my mother seemed to need me for moral support. I was torn between staying for their sake and leaving for my own good. I felt guilty about wanting to leave and expressed my dilemma to one of my close friends. She suggested that I talk to a psychologist she had heard speak at a Marriage Counseling class at her church. She offered to take me, since I didn't want my parents to know that I needed counseling. Actually, all I wanted was for someone to recommend that I should leave and not feel guilty about it.

Dr. Jeffries was a married man about 40 years old. As I entered his office, he pulled up a chair for me near his desk. I explained to him about my physical disabilities, and that he might have to help me to my feet when the session was over. He was very understanding and helped politely. The first three visits were great for my ego. After some psychological testing, he had me explain my situation. I confessed I was a little fearful about moving away. Even though I was walking now and taking care of myself, I still required help to get in and out of a car, to go up steps and sometimes to get up out of a chair. I would have to depend on the kindness of strangers in many situations. I also told him I felt guilty about leaving my parents but that I wanted a life of my own and hopefully someday to get married. The good doctor could not have been more encouraging. He was very kind and caring, and he said everything I wanted to hear. He said there was no reason why I couldn't manage the move, make friends, get a job and have a normal social life – even marriage.

On the fourth visit, I entered his office and he complimented me, saying how pretty I looked. He walked me over to a chair, and before I sat down, he suddenly put his arms around me, pulling me to him, and tried to kiss me. Horrified and embarrassed, I stepped back and fell into the chair. The sudden angry look on his face frightened me, and instead of confronting him about his actions, I thought it best to say nothing. I only wanted to get out of there, but my friend wouldn't be back for an hour.

He went to his desk, sat down and began looking over his notes. Finally, he looked up and said, *"Margaret, you need to face reality. Do you really expect strangers to be willing to go out of their way to help you? People don't mind sending a check to help needy or disabled people, but when it comes to touching a handicapped person, they consider it quite distasteful. I think you would be very lonely in Houston away from your family. And when it comes to marriage, I know you said that you have been dating someone, but no man would want to marry someone in your condition."* He went on tearing me down unmercifully. He pointed out everything negative about me he could think of – I had no training or education that would get me a job, no experience in the workforce and my physical disabilities would certainly be a detriment to my finding employment. He said I was emotionally weak and described difficult situations that I wouldn't be able to handle. My emotions went from fear to anger to disgust. He was trying to make me break down. I could see that he wanted to shatter any glimmer of hope that I had. Then he struck a lower blow. *"It's no wonder you feel guilty about leaving your parents. After all, they need you especially at this time of their lives. I really think you're being selfish."*

When the hour was up, I asked him to call my friend in from the waiting room. She chatted with him a minute. Then, I asked her, instead of the doctor, to help me up and we left. She could tell something was wrong but I never revealed to her what happened, knowing she would feel terrible for suggesting I see him.

For the next few days my mind played over and over all that Dr. Jeffries had said to me on my last visit. Finally, I came to my senses. In the first place, my going to him was ridiculous. I had wanted the approval and a push from a wise, ethical person. Who was this psychologist, anyway, but a stranger who cared nothing about me? He proved himself to be neither wise nor ethical. I already knew what my father, who loved me and knew what was best for me, would have advised me to do, had he not been old and sick. I knew because he had always encouraged me to find my own way in life and taught me not to be afraid to try. After all, my dad had left his family and his homeland when he was only fourteen. By leaving, he not only helped himself but was better able to help his family. I knew he didn't want me to be dependent on my brothers and sisters. I had to learn to live alone. It would be better for me and better for them as well.

My friend Beth in Houston helped me make arrangements to move in with a girl she knew. I told my parents I was going to Houston only for a visit and to see if I could do some more art work for the Medical Center. I couldn't bring myself to be upfront with them, but Mother seemed to perceive that I had more in my mind than just a visit. She looked me square in the eyes and said emphatically, *"Margaret, there is no way that you can possibly live away from home, so get that out of your head!"*

My brother Andrew drove me to Houston with the car packed up with all my gear, including two raised toilet seats, one for my apartment and the other for my prospective place of employment, and one straight ladder-back chair with a big cushion. These would take care of my sitting down and getting up problems.

So, I guess you could say that I ran away from home at the age of thirty.

Chapter 11

My roommate Patty was a pretty Jewish girl with dark hair, brown eyes and a cute personality. She had rented a two-bedroom apartment for us to share. She helped me get unpacked and set things up for my convenience. I searched the classified section of the newspaper every day and was optimistic about finding a job. Being on my own was gratifying as well as challenging. I learned to order the kinds of groceries that I could manage; for example, milk in half pint containers, small boxes of cereal and Oreo cookies. It took too much energy to try to cook. I didn't want to take advantage of Patty's kindness, nor did I want her to know how little I could do for myself. When my folks would call, my dad would always ask what I had eaten that day. I'd lie and describe a scrumptious meal so he wouldn't worry.

Two of Patty's friends came by one afternoon and we went out to eat together. On our return, as I was entering the apartment, I lost my balance and fell to the floor, breaking my left arm. The doctor in emergency said it would take at least six weeks for the break to heal. With my good arm in a sling, there was no way I could manage taking care of myself. Humbled and disappointed, I called my brother Andrew to come get me. I had left Dallas with such

In the Shadow of His Hand

determination and confidence but in less than a week I was back home.

My mom was sympathetic but relieved that I was home where she could watch over me. *"Now you see, Margaret,"* she said, *"that you cannot live on your own!"* I didn't tell her until my arm healed that I was planning to return to Houston. She had enough to be concerned about with my dad getting sicker. I knew that under the circumstances if I stayed in Dallas longer I would never be able to leave. Having had a taste of independence, I wasn't about to give it up. Dr. Jeffries wasn't altogether wrong when he said I was being selfish. In the long run it did turn out for the best for everyone concerned that I moved to Houston, but at the time my mother probably did need me, and I put my own interests first.

Once again my brother drove me to Houston. The very next morning I called the Texas Rehabilitation Center and made an appointment to talk to a counselor. One of their services was to find employment for the handicapped and assist them in any way they needed.

Patty kindly offered to take me to town for my appointment. I was interviewed by a Mr. Trilby, a young studious-looking man who had a PhD in something that was supposed to have qualified him for his position. He asked me three pages of questions pertaining to my physical disability and asked what work experience I had. I told him I had studied piano until I had polio. I explained my disabilities to him in detail, noting especially that I could use only one hand and it was very weak. I asked if he might find me a simple job in an office, perhaps answering the phone. When the interview was over, Patty came in and helped me up from the chair.

Mr. Trilby said he'd see what he could find and would call me. I waited by the phone for three days. When I finally heard from him, he had two very interesting job possibilities for me. One was as a file clerk and the other was as a piano player in a bar. *"Mr. Trilby, don't you understand?"* I asked incredulously. *"I'm not able to play the piano anymore; and as a file clerk I would have to carry the files around in my teeth!"* Sounding rather impatient, he said he would try to think of something else and would get back with me.

I waited a week, and then decided to go to the Texas Employment Commission. The counselor there suggested I could probably work as a proofreader. Hurray! Surely, I could do that, since I did know how to read and could spell fairly well. She promised to let me know as soon as a proofreading job became available. In the meantime, I looked in the Yellow Pages and called several printing and typesetting companies. I almost fainted when I found such a job opening and was asked to come in for an interview the next day! *"Oh, dear,"* I thought to myself, *"What do I do now?"* Patty would be at work and wouldn't be able to take me. A dozen more questions came to mind. What if there were several steps to get into the building? Would I be able to sit down for an interview and get up without having to ask the boss for help? What if the restrooms were inaccessible? Then I remembered Mr. Trilby, PhD, who had been no help to me thus far. This fellow needed to earn his pay.

He was somewhat taken aback when I informed him I had found a job opening and needed him to drive me to the interview. *"You mean you have an interview tomorrow?"* he asked in amazement. *"Yes, and I need you to take me,"* I replied. He hesitated, mumbling something about it not being the proper procedure. I reminded him he was supposed to help the handicapped become gainfully employed and if he didn't help me I would lose this job

In the Shadow of His Hand

opportunity. Since I found the job by myself, something he had been unable to do, surely he could help me get to the interview. He reluctantly agreed to take me.

When Mr. Trilby picked me up the next morning I asked him if he would mind carrying the box which contained my raised toilet seat. It was a little embarrassing for me to ask him, but I knew I would need to take it along in case I got the job. We left it in the car until I had my interview.

Everything went exceedingly well. Little details that most people wouldn't notice were gigantic benefits for me. The company was located in a small one-story building. The curb outside the building was only about two inches high, easy enough for me to step up. Once inside, the secretary led me into the office to meet the big boss. He offered me a chair but I said I would rather stand. He asked me how much college I had and I told him I had studied English, French, Spanish and Greek but that I had only two years of college. I wasn't about to tell him I quit after one semester of English. My thinking? A little deception is okay if the cause is good. Oh, how easy it was for me to try to justify the sins of my young adulthood! Actually, the boss was easy-going and would rather have been out on the golf course. He probably would have hired me even if I had told the truth, but I was taking no chances. After all, I was depending on "luck" and I wasn't sure how far "luck" would take me. *The job is yours starting tomorrow,"* he said. He led me into a large room where all the work took place, showed me my desk which was near the door and asked me to sit there to fill out some papers. Amazingly, the chair at the desk had been left swiveled up to exactly the height I needed. Getting up was no problem! On my way out I checked out the bathroom facilities and explained to the receptionist that I would be bringing in a couple of items that I needed because of my

69

"slight" physical disability. Then, I asked Mr. Trilby to bring in "the box" and place it next to the wall by the toilet.

After he helped me into the car, I told him I needed him to take me to Sears. I don't know where my sudden boldness came from, but I knew this was not the time to be shy. *"What on earth for?"* he asked, looking quite astonished. *"I need a small piece of carpet to put under the desk chair because the floor was a little slippery,"* I explained. *"But I can't do that,"* he protested. *"But you must, or I might fall trying to get up. I have no other way of getting it if you don't take me,"* I insisted. Finally, he relented and took me to the store. After purchasing a small rug I persuaded Mr. Trilby to take me back to the printing company and place the rug on the floor under my desk chair. On the way back to my apartment, he complained about all the driving he had done, so I offered to pay for the gas and thanked him profusely for all his help. He refused to take the money but he seemed very exasperated and said, *"You know, you rushed me into this before I had a chance to get a doctor's report saying that you really do have a physical disability!"* I almost laughed. *"What do you mean? Do you think I've been pretending all this time?"* I asked. *"I guess not,"* he said, *"but I'm supposed to have your disability verified by a physician!"* *"Well,"* I responded, *"All I know is, I've got the job! And if we had waited for that little detail, the job probably would have gone to someone else."*

Chapter 12

Feeling like a *"Thoroughly Modern Millie"*, I entered into the world of the American working girl. Patty drove me back and forth to work at first but it was several miles out of her way. I got the idea to call a church that was right across the street from our apartment and asked if there was anyone in their congregation that I could possibly car pool with to downtown Houston. A nice lady called me back and arrangements were made. Of course, I couldn't share the driving but I could share the gasoline expense. She was nice about helping me in and out the car. One cold and windy winter evening when she brought me home from work, I was a little apprehensive about walking by myself from the parking area to my apartment but decided I could make it. As I stepped around the corner of the building, however, a blast of cold air hit me and I fell backwards into a flower bed, landing in between some bushes. Thankfully, my heavy coat cushioned my fall and my head hit the dirt. I knew I would either have to scream for help, as embarrassing as that would be, or lie there and freeze to death. So, I began to yell! Finally, a man came out of his apartment, looked around and saw my feet sticking out onto the sidewalk. He helped me up, introduced himself and walked me to my door. Whenever I saw him at the apartment complex get-

Sarah Margaret Smith

togethers, he would laughingly tell the neighbors how he found me lying in the flower bed one day!

Every day was a new experience. I took my first taxi ride to a nearby beauty shop. I felt rather leery about asking the cabdriver to lift my legs for me into the vehicle, lift them out when we got there and also help me to my feet. My parents would have had apoplexy had they known the chances I was taking.

Getting up early, getting myself dressed and then working all day was exhausting. After work I would fall onto the bed to rest for a couple of hours before I could even think about eating anything. I eventually got used to the routine. My muscles, apparently, had reached their peak of improvement and were not getting any stronger, but my endurance was increasing. I began trying to eat a more nutritious diet, ordering groceries that were easy to prepare. For example, I would have the butcher cut up steak into bite-size pieces for me. I would broil it in my counter top toaster oven and bake a small potato to eat with it.

After a few months my parents realized that I was not just visiting my girlfriend, but that I had actually moved to Houston. I would ride the Greyhound bus home at least one weekend a month to see them. The bus driver would have to carry me up the steps onto the bus.

Soon after I moved in with Patty, she told me she had undergone heart surgery the year before because of some rare congenital heart disease that I didn't really understand. The famous heart surgeon Dr. Denton Cooley explained that surgery could correct the problem for a time but the condition probably would return eventually. In the meantime, Patty was trying to enjoy life to the fullest. She and her boyfriend were hoping for the best and planned to get married the next year.

In the Shadow of His Hand

Nine months later Patty married. I moved into a one-bedroom apartment to live alone for the first time. I became friends with two girls who lived next door. We enjoyed each other's company and they helped me whenever I needed something. Patty would come by often and I could see that she was blissfully happy. After less than six weeks of marriage, however, she began having problems again with her heart. Dr. Cooley informed her that there was a very slight chance another surgery could help but it would be extremely risky. Without the surgery she would have only a few months to live. Patty opted to have the surgery but first she wanted to travel to North Carolina to visit her family there. She seemed to know she would be seeing them for the last time. When she and her husband returned, she checked into the hospital. She called to tell me and I went to see her. She was weak and very afraid. It came to my mind that here she was, a dying Jew, and I, supposedly, a Christian. One of the few theological truths I knew anything about was that only Christians go to heaven when they die, but I could find no words to explain something that I didn't really understand.

It was disturbing to me that I had nothing to say to my dying friend, and a blow to my pride that I could not explain something I had always professed to be.

Death remained a sad and morbid inevitability. Patty, frightened and seemingly without hope, died on the operating table. At her funeral, I was stunned and further dismayed to learn that Patty had not been born Jewish. She was a Gentile, raised a Methodist, and had only recently denounced Christianity and converted to Judaism.

***

By early November of 1965, my dad's emphysema was getting worse. I received a phone call at work from my mother. *"Margaret, you've got to come home,"* she insisted. *"Your father is sick and you need to be here."* I told my boss and he granted me an extended leave of absence. I left the next day for Dallas.

I was glad to be home again. Although my dad was rapidly declining, on his better days he would sit in his recliner on the glassed in patio where he could enjoy the view of the backyard flower garden. Red bougainvillea he had planted and nurtured decorated the white wrought iron trellis that framed the glass windows. Mother and I would take turns sitting and talking with him, and, of course, my brothers and sisters would come by often. My uncle Haralambos and his daughter had been visiting from Greece for several months and my dad was able to enjoy having his brother with him during those last days of his life.

For as long as I could remember, my father had been terrified of dying. Whenever he had the flu or a bad cold, he would lie in bed moaning and calling out in Greek, *"Ach, Mana mou,"* to his deceased mother, thinking this was surely the dreaded end. But now, suddenly, when his death was near and he *knew* it, he seemed very peaceful. This was strikingly out of character for him and I puzzled over it. Even though his breathing was shallow and speaking was tiring, he was not at all fretful or afraid. Then, for reasons I didn't know, he had my mother remove the religious pictures depicting the apostles Andrew and John from the top of the bureau in the bedroom.

For there is one God, and one mediator between God and men, the man Christ Jesus.

1 Timothy 2:5

On the morning of December 13, 1965, we gathered around my father's bed, knowing that the end was imminent. He had slipped into a coma and his face was ashen. It looked as if his life was being kept only by the pumping of the breathing machine. The doctor arrived and, after examining him, removed the breathing mask and turned off the machine. He then gave him a shot of something that seemed to revive him and brought color back into his face. I thought to myself, *"He's going to be okay!"* But after a few restful moments his breathing stopped and the spirit of this formerly vibrant energetic man left his body. Where it went, I didn't know for sure, but for the first time I became convinced that there is life after death.

It was a difficult time, especially for my mother. When she began considering selling the house and moving into an apartment, I asked her if I should stay or go back to Houston. Realizing that I had started a new life, she encouraged me to go. Six weeks later I returned to Houston.

Chapter 13

My carpooling friend had changed jobs and was no longer able to take me to work, but I heard about a new high-rise apartment building downtown called the Houston House, not far from my job. It had a coffee shop, a nice restaurant and private club, a small commissary and a beauty shop. On top of all those amenities, it would cost only fifty-five cents to take a cab to work from there each day. It seemed perfect for me, so I rented an apartment. It was a little more expensive than what I had been paying, but well worth it, considering the conveniences it offered.

The slick terrazzo floors in the lobby and throughout the first floor caused me to walk very cautiously and close to the wall. Also, I was petrified about getting on the elevator, but I had to do it. I would wait till someone else was getting on and ask them to hold the door and push the button for me. My apartment was on the 22nd floor. If the elevator was empty when I reached my floor, I would hold my breath and get out as fast as I could, hoping the door wouldn't close on me and knock me down.

I explained to the doorman at the Houston House my need for assistance getting in and out of taxis, and he very graciously offered to help me each day. He would even explain to the cabdriver how to help me once I reached my

In the Shadow of His Hand

destination. This worked out fine. The cabdrivers would drive me to work, help me out and walk me to the door of the building. However, one cabdriver, a short chubby little man, refused to help me out of his taxi. I was about to ask him to go inside and ask one of my co-workers to come help when he began to wave his arms and shout to two men who were high up on a scaffold, painting the outside of the building. *"Hey, Painters, Painters,"* he yelled. *"Come down here! Come get this lady out of my cab! I can't get her out!"* People on the street turned and stared as the two men hurried down with their paint buckets splashing and looking as if they were about to see a dead or mangled body in the backseat. *"Oh, hi,"* I said cheerfully as they opened the door and peered in at me. Trying to overcome my embarrassment, I added, *"I'm really okay. I just need some help. Would you mind lifting my legs out and then help me stand up?"*

One Saturday morning I felt brave enough to go down to the coffee shop/commissary to buy a couple of items. As I walked to the cash register my foot slipped out from under me because of some water that someone had spilt. I fell straight backwards and cracked my head on the terrazzo floor. The manager called an ambulance and I was taken to emergency to be stitched up. I could almost depend on having a bad fall now and then.

Many single adults lived in the building but I knew no one. My co-workers were nice and I liked them, but most of them were married or lived far out from the city. I did meet Adele who worked at the front desk at the Houston House. She was very helpful when I moved into my apartment.

I came home early from my job one afternoon sick with chills and fever. I stopped at the front desk to get my mail and mentioned to Adele that I wasn't feeling well. She called to see how I was doing before she left work. Her thoughtfulness surprised me since I didn't know her very well. My fever had gone down after taking some aspirin and I assured her that I was fine. She was going out on a dinner date and told me she'd call me the next morning. I went to sleep and woke up around nine o'clock that evening gasping for breath. I called my polio friend Beth to get the name of her doctor. It was all I could do to get the words out. She could barely hear me. She called her doctor for me and he advised that I should go to Methodist Hospital and he would meet me there. In the meantime, my breathing was getting worse and I was frightened. Speaking was becoming more difficult and I needed to call an ambulance but couldn't find the strength. I desperately needed help but I didn't know what to do. About that time I heard a knock at the door. I was unable to answer but in a minute I heard the door unlock and in walked Adele. Obviously, the Lord wasn't ready for me to meet my death and, therefore, put it into the mind of this woman whom I barely knew to come to my aid. Little did I know that guardian angels were hovering over me and that God was preserving me for future purposes.

Are they (the angels) not all ministering spirits,

sent fort to minister for them who shall be

heirs of salvation?

Hebrews1:14

Suddenly, during her dinner Adele had become worried about me and explained to her date that she needed to drop by the Houston House to check on a friend. She used

In the Shadow of His Hand

her pass key to get in my apartment. As soon as she saw me she called the house doctor (I didn't know the Houston House had a house doctor). He took one look at me and called an ambulance. *"What about your family, Margaret?"* Adele asked. I whispered, *"Call ... Chris,"* and pointed to my address book on the nightstand. Chris immediately made arrangements to come to Houston. That, of course, would take several hours. When the ambulance came, the doctor instructed the driver and his assistant, neither of whom were paramedics, to give me oxygen to sustain me on the way to the hospital. Adele insisted on riding in the ambulance with me.

As soon as we drove off, Adele asked the driver about the oxygen. *"Oh, we don't have any oxygen,"* he admitted, *"but she'll probably be okay, don'tcha think?"* I was already struggling for breath, and when I heard his words I became more anxious. Adele tried to get me to relax, coaxing me to be calm and to take slow shallow breaths, realizing that any anxiety would make my breathing even more difficult. I remember looking at the window where the name of the company was printed. Making out the name, reading it backwards from the inside of the ambulance, I thought to myself, *"If I get out of this alive I'm going to report these guys!"* There were many complaints in Houston around that time against several private ambulance companies, and I understood why. It's no wonder the fire department soon took over all ambulance service in the city.

The doctor at Methodist concluded that I had the flu which had settled in my larynx and esophagus, and a touch of pneumonia. After several days in the hospital, I went back to my apartment to convalesce for two weeks.

Chris stayed a couple of days and then my mother came down to be with me until I got better.

Chapter 14

Not having many friends, I was lonely. An idea came to me. I put a sign up in the laundry area saying, "Anyone interested in taking Spanish lessons, call Margaret," and I gave my phone number. Soon, eight people signed up for the class, five women and three men. All I had to do next was find a teacher! I called the YWCA and asked if they offered Spanish classes, and they did. I spoke to the teacher and asked if she would consider teaching a class one evening a week at my apartment. She was delighted when I told her I had eight people already signed up.

Through these eight people I met others who lived in the apartment building, and no longer felt all alone in a strange place. My social life definitely picked up and for the next four years I enjoyed meeting new people, dating occasionally, and going to parties. It was a fun time and, of course, unusual incidents were often happening to me.

I became friends with Ruth Parker, a widow in her late fifties, who lived at the Houston House. She would often drop by after work. We'd practice our Spanish and visit a while. She spoke very highly about her son Wilson, who was a Marine serving in Vietnam. When he came home on leave she eagerly brought him over to meet me. Wilson was nice looking and very polite. The next day he called and

In the Shadow of His Hand

asked me out. Feeling perfectly at ease to go out with him, – after all, I knew his mother – I accepted the invitation. We had a nice dinner at a nearby restaurant and then he suggested we drive out to the popular Greek place down by the ship channel. I'd been there before and enjoyed the food and the Greek music. Houstonians would flock there to watch the sailors from the Greek ships in port dance to the live *bouzoukia* music. As soon as we were seated, Wilson ordered a bottle of wine and proceeded to guzzle it down. After drinking half of a second bottle of wine, he went out to the car and brought in a bottle of whiskey. I began to worry about getting home safely. It was getting late and Wilson was visibly intoxicated. When I suggested he order some coffee to drink, he became angry, pounded the table, picked up the half bottle of wine and poured it all over me. I was frightened. With the loud music and low lighting, no one even noticed my plight. About that time Costas, the manager, happened over to our table. With a forced smile on my face I introduced him to Wilson. Then, switching to Greek but maintaining my smile, I explained that I was terrified and needed his help to get me up and away from my date. The rest of the evening was much like a slapstick comedy. Costas, with typical Greek gallantry, took the situation in hand. He explained politely to Wilson that because it was after hours no opened bottles of liquor were allowed on the tables and that he would have to take the whiskey out to his car. Wilson complied begrudgingly and the minute he was out the door Costas helped me to my feet and rushed me into the kitchen where I hid between a large freezer and a tall cabinet. With waiters hurrying back and forth carrying large trays of food, I would peek around the cabinet and see Wilson charging through the swinging doors into the kitchen searching for me, with the manager following right behind him insisting that I wasn't there. He

Sarah Margaret Smith

ushered him out of the kitchen several times while I ducked behind the freezer. Finally, I noticed a telephone on the kitchen wall and called a friend at the Houston House, briefed him on the situation and asked him to come rescue me. When my friend arrived Costas brought him into the kitchen and let us out a back door. Thus, we safely eluded the enraged Wilson.

***

No matter how hard I tried to be careful and sensible, harrowing experiences seemed to keep happening to me. I would often ride the elevator up with a nice older gentleman, Mr. Corelli, who lived across the hall. Apparently, he loved sports because his cronies would gather frequently at his apartment and they'd have the television blaring the football games and other sports events. One Saturday afternoon during the Christmas holidays he invited everyone on our floor to an "open house" at his apartment. A married couple I knew was going, so I joined them. I sat on the couch with them while drinks and hors d'oeuvres were served, and chatted with other neighbors who dropped by. I thought it strange that even during the party two televisions were on and some of the men were keeping track of the scores of various ballgames. Also, the telephone was constantly ringing. Guests would come, stay a while and go. Suddenly, I realized that the couple I came with had left; in fact, everyone I was acquainted with was leaving. I needed someone to help me up so I could leave, but only a few men were left, men that I didn't know, and they were in the kitchen having a heated argument about money. I heard threats and cursing, and the phone kept ringing. It finally dawned on me that Mr. Corelli was a *bookie*! He would have brief telephone conversations and hang up abruptly.

In the Shadow of His Hand

Then I heard him say to the other men, *"They're coming up here!"* I feared I was about to witness a physical confrontation if not a shooting; or maybe it was the police coming to arrest everyone there, including me! I quickly found the courage to ask one of the men as he passed through the living room to help me up and out the door I went. With my heart pounding and my hands shaking, I locked myself in my apartment. The next day Mr. Corelli was gone and his apartment was completely vacated!

At the time, I thought these years were important for expanding my horizons and finding out who I was. That was the big thing back in the 60s – finding out who you were. But, actually, becoming independent and part of the social scene drew me more into the modern world with its subtle but growing new-age influences and frivolous values. Partying and gaiety, although entertaining, did nothing for the soul. Without the under-girding of faith and the guiding principles of God's Word, I was adrift like a ship without an anchor.

As the wise King Solomon wrote in the Bible:

I said in my heart, "Come now, I will test you with mirth; therefore enjoy pleasure"; but surely, this also was vanity. I said of laughter—"Madness!"; and of mirth, "What does it accomplish?" I searched in my heart how to gratify my flesh with wine, while guiding my heart with wisdom, and how to lay hold on folly, till I might see what was good for the sons of men to do under heaven all the days of their lives. Vanity of vanities ... All is vanity.

Ecclesiastes 2: 1-3, 12: 8 NKJ

There was a definite void in my life. At times, I attributed it to homesickness or to my longing to find the love of my life and be married, but it was more than that. An underlying feeling of uncertainty would gnaw at me occasionally and with the uncertainty came a sense of guilt.

In an effort to feel better about myself I began taking classes at church where I was given religious instruction. With a portion of my time being given to religion, I dismissed my feelings of guilt and considered that my life was now in proper order, unaware that none of the instruction had touched on my real spiritual need.

Was I searching for God? No, not really. My emptiness was evidence of my *need* for God, but my *searching* was for a good feeling about myself and for confidence that I was meeting the requirements for being a *"good"* person. In my confusion I was looking to myself and what I could do to cleanse my soul, rather than looking to the Lord.

In the Shadow of His Hand

Not by works of righteousness which we have done, but according to His mercy He saved us, by the washing of regeneration and renewing of the Holy Spirit.

Titus 3:5 NKJ

For by grace are ye saved through faith; and that, not of yourselves. It is the gift of God, not of works, lest any man should boast.

Ephesians 2:8-9

***

A very nice lady who lived at the Houston House invited me over one afternoon for coffee and began talking about the importance of being "in tune with the spirits." She went into great detail saying how the spirits guided her and gave her insight into the future. I wasn't sure what she meant until she brought out a deck of Tarot cards and began telling my fortune. In earlier days my sisters and I had gone to a fortune teller just for a lark. It was fun but I found it a bit too spooky and the things that were said played on my mind for weeks. As curious as I was about the future, I wasn't drawn in to this lady's practice of divination with the cards, not because I was wise, but because I knew I would worry about anything the least bit sinister she might tell me. I did enough worrying already, without adding her mystical predictions to my mind.

Therefore, I avoided her company and contented myself with a supposed confidence that I had everything I needed.

A young woman from the Spanish class often asked me to go with her and her friends out to eat or to sports events. Her name was Mary Archer. One day she came over to visit after work. She asked me to go to dinner with her and her boyfriend who was coming by to pick her up. After I agreed, she asked if I would mind if we rode in his truck. *"Of course not, no problem,"* I said. Thinking it would be a light-weight pickup and that I would probably need just a little boost to get into it, I was stunned when I saw the vehicle. It was a huge commercial dump truck! The seat was at least six feet off the ground. Her friend, a large jovial fellow, whisked me up in his arms, lifted me almost above his head and tossed me onto the front seat. I thought to myself, *"How do I get into these situations?"* In order to avoid being hoisted in and out any more than necessary, I suggested we bring hamburgers back to the apartment instead of going to a restaurant.

A few weeks later, persistent Mary invited me to a party that she and some friends were having. It was to be held in a large reception room of a downtown motor hotel. There would be music and dancing, but, of course, I couldn't dance. I really didn't want to go but she insisted, refusing to take no for an answer. I consented, only after she promised we would go in her car and *not* a dump truck.

In the Shadow of His Hand

She drove me to the party and as we were approaching the entrance of the hotel, a man she had invited to the event walked up and greeted her. Mary introduced him to me. His name was Glenn Smith. He was tall with thick wavy black hair, broad shoulders and rugged good looks. Mary had met him at the hospital where she worked and they often had coffee together on their breaks. He was the plumbing superintendent in the construction of a new wing of the hospital. When she asked him to the party he also reluctantly accepted the invitation. Glenn noticed her take my arm to help me up a step and immediately offered his assistance. He was not only handsome, but thoughtful and considerate. He spent the entire evening sitting with me while others were dancing. In fact, he was very protective. When another young man approached and asked me to dance, grabbing my hand as if he were about to playfully jerk me up out of my chair, Glenn quickly perceived the potential harm to me, and forcibly removed the man's hand from mine, explaining that I was unable to dance. My hero from the very beginning!

The evening went well and we enjoyed getting acquainted, talking and laughing together. He also had a serious side and revealed a depth of character I found so often lacking in other men I had met. Unpretentious and straightforward, he told me he was divorced and spoke at length about his two young daughters. I could sense his deep love for them and his pain at not having them live with him.

When the evening was over, Glenn said he would call me and I hoped he would. I was terribly attracted to him.

Weeks went by, then months without hearing from him and I assumed he had forgotten about me.

In September of 1968, almost a year later, he called. Although I was surprised to hear from him after such a long time, my mind raced back to the enjoyable evening we had spent together and I was glad to hear his voice. He asked me out but, unfortunately, I was recovering from another bout with pneumonia. I asked him to call back in two weeks. Again, weeks went by without hearing from him. Finally, he called after Christmas and we had our first date on January 8, 1969.

Even though I had begun to think that Glenn really wasn't interested in going out with me, after that first date we saw each other as often as possible. How can one describe love? We didn't just "fall" in love by accident. We saw love in each other's eyes, we heard love in each other's words and we felt love in each other's touch.

I admired his being such a loving father to his two children; in fact, I loved everything about him. Each evening when we went out together, he would remember to call his daughters and talk with them a few minutes. He would often bring them over on Saturdays. The girls were fun and I enjoyed them. Terri, fourteen, was pretty with blue eyes and beautiful black wavy hair like her dad's. Dana at twelve was a cute freckle-faced redhead, later blossoming into a lovely young lady. She was part tomboy and part comedienne.

Glenn proposed to me in April and I happily accepted. Before I had a chance to announce our engagement to my family, my older sister Sophie and her husband came to Houston for a visit. I told my sister about Glenn and that he had proposed. She seemed a little apprehensive about meeting him. That evening we all went out to dinner together and had a great time. I could tell they liked Glenn.

By the end of the evening Sophie took me aside and said, *"Marry him, Margaret, he's great!"* Pleased that she liked him, I answered, *"I'm going to!"*

Glenn and Margaret are engaged

We married July 17, 1969. Mother had wanted to give us a nice wedding in Dallas but at that time I could tell she wasn't up to it physically. I convinced her that we could get married in Houston, and then she could give us a reception in Dallas when she was feeling better. Actually, the thought of having a big wedding never appealed to me and I was quite relieved when Mother agreed to my suggestion. So, without the usual fuss and frustration of wedding arrangements, Glenn and I said our vows in a private ceremony in a church in Houston. It couldn't have been more special. In fact, I got so emotional that even Glenn and the preacher teared up! Later in Dallas, Mother gave us a beautiful wedding dinner at the Chaparral Club and a reception at the Park Towers.

Chapter 15

We bought a home in southwest Houston and I gladly quit my job a few months later to become a full-time homemaker. I'd walk from room to room gazing around and thinking, *"Can this be real or am I dreaming?"* I was as happy as a little girl playing house. I loved being at home. Glenn was thoughtful and understanding about my inability to do much housecleaning and soon we hired a maid to come in weekly.

Knowing nothing about interior decorating, I kept putting off buying new furniture. Finally, one day Glenn decided to take me and our younger daughter Dana to a furniture store. When he dropped us off he said, *"I'll be back in half an hour. That'll be long enough for you to buy living room furniture, right?"* This was my first clue that men are fast shoppers.

On our first trip to a large department store Glenn thought it best that I use my wheelchair. After pushing me up and down every aisle of every department of the three level store, whizzing along at record speed, darting around and passing other shoppers like a speedster on the freeway, he asked as we were leaving, *"Why didn't you buy anything?"* *"Oh, I really didn't see anything I wanted,"* I replied.

90

In the Shadow of His Hand

Me, in my very own kitchen!

I set my mind to learn how to cook. I began trying out recipes from my cookbook and made many long-distance phone calls to Chris in Dallas for help.

Glenn was definitely a meat and potatoes man but I eventually introduced him to vegetables. He came home from the grocery store one day with a rolled roast. I had never seen a rolled roast and the next day when I started to cook it, I cut the strings off that were holding it together, thinking they'd burn. Quickly realizing that was the wrong thing to do, but having no other string in the house, I used the next best thing – sewing thread, winding it around and around and around. I followed a recipe for pot roast and was delighted with the delectable aroma that filled the house. When it was done I cut the threads and tried my best to remove them all. That evening as Glenn eagerly served our plates I noticed pieces of thread swimming in the gravy. Hoping he wouldn't notice, I said nothing but waited for his comment. *"This is really good,"* he said, *"and you know, you can floss your teeth while you're eating it!"*

I bought every kind of kitchen gadget I could find in order to make life easier. The onion chopper, however, didn't work out so well. Having put large chunks of onion into the cup-like container and attaching the top that had a plunger, I found that my arm was not strong enough to press the bladed plunger down. So, I leaned over and used my chin, banging it down again and again on the plunger! This worked out fine. But I woke up one morning with a large painful lump under my chin. Thinking it might be some kind of tumor I started to make an appointment with the doctor. Then the cause of the problem finally occurred to me. Chopping onions with my chin!

For Christmas that first year our Dana gave me a hand-held electric vegetable peeler. I could hardly wait to try it out. Unable to hold the potato in one hand and the peeler in the other, I placed the potato in the sink and chased it around with the electric peeler like a mad woman. Before I knew it there were potato peelings everywhere – on the wall, all over the counter and in my hair! The poor potato was rather mutilated, but it was definitely peeled. Glenn came in from work before I had a chance to clean up the mess. Later, for obvious reasons, he instructed me not to ever use the electric knife.

One rainy morning after Glenn left for work, I decided to take a whole chicken out of the freezer. It was in a plastic bag held closed with a twisty. Knowing it was too heavy for me to lift out with my hand, I clenched my teeth around the closed end of the bag, lifted it out of the freezer and carried it hanging from my mouth toward the sink. Unfortunately, I dropped it right on the toes of my left foot.

In the Shadow of His Hand

Thinking I must have broken a toe, I hobbled to the telephone to call Glenn to come home. I found the name of an orthopedist and made an appointment to see him right away. By the time we got to the doctor's office it was raining hard, and, of course, we were not wearing raincoats. We were able to park near the door of the medical building and I walked in, limping along. After looking at my foot, the doctor said he doubted that it was broken but that I should have an x-ray taken. That was fine, except he had no x-ray machine in his office. He sent all his patients across the street to the hospital for x-rays. This, too, would've been okay but by now the rain had turned into a monsoon. The hospital was crowded and since we had to park quite a way from the door, Glenn decided to pick me up and carry me from the car into the hospital. Drenched to the skin and looking like we had just washed up on shore, we were escorted to the x-ray department. Once the x-rays were taken, we were informed we would have to take the films with us *back* to the doctor's office to get the report. With the winds now reaching almost hurricane force along with the blinding rain, Glenn made his way to the car and brought it to the entrance of the hospital. We drove back to the medical building, and my dear husband, breathing heavily, carried me again, this time from the car to the doctor's office. When we saw the doctor, he said, *"Well, your toe was not broken, but even if it had been there's nothing we would've done about it."* Stunned, Glenn asked, *"So, are you telling me that our trip in this storm to the hospital was really not necessary?"* *"Well,"* the doctor answered, *"I assumed you wanted to know whether or not her toe was broken."*

I promised Glenn I would never again carry a frozen chicken in my teeth.

***

Glenn owned a beach house on the Bolivar peninsula overlooking the Gulf of Mexico. It was a fun place to go on the weekends and often we'd take the girls and their friends along. We'd drive from Houston to Galveston and take the ferry across to Bolivar. The house was up on stilts and Glenn would have to carry me up the flight of stairs. I loved going to the beach in the early morning when the sun was rising. We'd watch the color of the ocean change from the black of night to a shimmering silver at pre-dawn. Then, as the sun peered through the low-lying morning clouds above the horizon, blushes of pinks and reds would cast their glow on the water. In the late afternoons we would relax out on the deck or go down to watch the seiners drag in their huge nets filled with all kinds of fish. Glenn would fish in the surf, sometimes all night. He'd wake me up and hold a speckled trout or redfish over my head, proudly displaying his catch.

Besides his regular work, Glenn continued his part-time job of umpiring baseball several evenings out of the month – everything from Little League to college ball. Having been quite an athlete in his younger years, he liked being involved with sports. Sometimes I'd go along and watch. This activity, however, came to an end when he suffered a knee injury and had to have surgery. I was petrified he might die on the operating table and I'd lose the love of my life, but he came through it just fine. When they rolled him back into the room, I stood at his bedside until he woke up. As the nurse was adjusting his pillows, trying to make him comfortable, I began feeling weak. The nurse noticed the color draining from my face and got to me just as I fainted! She called out for assistance and other nurses and orderlies came running, hovering over me while poor Glenn was left unattended, moaning in pain. Once he was home, as much as I wanted to be "Nancy Nurse," it turned out that my efforts only caused more problems. For example, when I slowly and carefully brought him a cup of soup from the kitchen, I ended up spilling it all over the bed. Swallowing my pride, I finally sent out an SOS to Glenn's dad who came and stayed with us until Glenn was on his feet.

Chapter 16

Here I was at age thirty five, the stepmother of two young teenage girls and I didn't have a clue about step-parenting. I didn't know if I should act like a mother or a friend, so I tried to be a little bit of both because they seemed to need it and expect it. Terri, who turned fifteen a month after we married, was quite grown up for her age. She was busy working part-time jobs and going out with her friends on the weekends, which gave us less time to be with her. Dana, on the other hand, was with us almost every weekend. She would cling to us when it was time to say goodbye. The broken home situation seemed to be more difficult for her than for Terri. Dana was still her daddy's little girl.

The cultural change during the late 60s and early 70s was shocking and disturbing to most caring parents as it spread its influence like a tidal wave on society, especially on the young. I could see its effect even on our girls. The lyrics of the popular rock songs encouraged profanity, rebellion, social protest, sex and drugs.

Although I was extremely happy in my marriage, uncertainty continued to trouble me at times, especially in regard to the girls. Because of my pride I wanted to have all the right answers and to be confident in my judgments, but I was in unfamiliar territory. Glenn and I were together in our

96

In the Shadow of His Hand

opinions on morality and social behavior, and wanted desperately to encourage the girls in the right direction. We realized we should at least be taking them to church on Sundays. After all, most nice people go to church and we wanted them to have nice friends. We began visiting various churches but had not settled on any one of them when my longtime friend Harriet called and invited me to go with her to a women's Bible class that was going to be held at her neighbor's house. (Harriet married and moved to Houston not long after our adventurous trip to Greece together. She was now the mother of four children.) I had never attended a Bible study of any kind. On occasion, I had tried to read the Bible but it had never touched me personally, and I couldn't get much out of it. However, being aware of my inadequacies as a step parent, I readily accepted her invitation when she told me it would be a non-denominational study with subjects such as marriage and child rearing being discussed. The morning of the class I located my Bible on the bookshelf, dusted it off and waited for Harriet to pick me up.

It was a warm friendly group of approximately fifteen women. They were going through a book called *The Christian Home.* The chapter that day was an overview of the Christian home, and every word of instruction was backed up with Scripture. The leader of the group would read a paragraph and then invite discussion about it. I was amazed that these women actually used the Bible as a guide to live by. They faced many of the same kinds of difficulties in life that most people face, but they knew where to go for the answers. They took God's Word seriously and believed it.

I left there realizing that they had something I didn't have. For one thing, most of them had some knowledge of the Bible. Another thing that surprised me was that the Scriptures that we read were relevant to our modern day and to my life personally. I told Glenn all about it when I got home. *"I've been a Christian all my life,"* or so I thought, *"and I don't know anything about the Bible."* He suggested I ask the women where they went to church and perhaps we could visit.

As it turned out, they attended various churches – some denominational and some non-denominational. We decided to visit a church near our neighborhood where one of the ladies in the class and her husband were members.

After an opening prayer, several hymns were sung. Then, the preacher began reading and teaching from the Gospel of John. It was all about Jesus, the Good Shepherd and only Savior, and His love for His sheep. I was deeply moved and my eyes filled with tears. I didn't fully understand everything but I was convinced that this was what I needed – *God's Word.*

I began reading the Bible at home and the words seemed to jump off the pages and into my heart. I read about Jesus being the Light of the world and I realized I had been walking in spiritual darkness all my life. No wonder I had been plagued with uncertainty.

I am the Light of the world;

he who followeth me shall not walk in darkness,

but shall have the light of life.

John 8:12

When the Lord brings light to the blind eyes of one of His lost sheep, He also gives a thirst for the Scriptures. It was through the Scriptures that I began to learn about God, and about myself. I learned, also, that there was nothing I could do to atone for my sins. I became convicted of the transgressions that I had always tried to justify. Not only my outward sins, but the sins of pride, covetousness and self-centeredness came into my mind and condemned me. Mostly, I was ashamed of my hypocrisy. Having professed for years that I was a Christian, I had never followed Christ. Although I had acknowledged Him as the Son of God, I never desired to live my life according to His Word. Beautiful religious music could move me to tears at times, but my heart was not filled with praise and love for the Lord. It was only through the working of the Holy Spirit that I was awakened to see Christ as my Lord and Savior.

By His Grace

A token nod to God I gave,
But trusted not His Written Word.
Confusion, doubts and fears prevailed
While on Life's path I blindly raced.

Then Truth descended to my heart
And shattered self, revealed my pride.
Arrested, guilty of my sin,
"It's Christ I need!" I cried.

But as the Sword of Truth cut deep,
God's mercy followed as a balm
To show me that Christ died for me,
And drew me to the Beloved One.

S. M. Smith

Although an undeserving sinner, I found complete forgiveness in Christ. I was no longer burdened with the weight of my sin. All my uncertainties were replaced with confidence in the Lord and in His Word. The emptiness in my soul was filled with peace.

Therefore being justified by faith, we have

peace with God through our

Lord Jesus Christ.

Romans 5:1

I remember a picture I painted several years before I moved to Houston. It depicted a long dark hallway that led to a partially opened door. The light, shining through the opening of the door, was warm and inviting. I don't know why I decided on such a subject, but I remember thinking when I finished it, *"This is the way life seems to be. You go along in the dark, and hope that someday you might get to a place of contentment."*

But Jesus said,

I am come a light into the world, that whosoever

believeth on me

should not abide in darkness.

John 12:46

Chapter 17

With new joy in my heart, I busied myself with the daily routine of cooking and whatever light household chores I could do. Glenn and I looked forward to church each Sunday and we also attended a midweek Bible class where we made lots of new friends. Each morning at home, I was drawn to the Scriptures and to prayer in a special quiet time with the Lord. Sensing His presence throughout the day, however, I realized I could turn to Him at any time.

Thou art my hiding place and my shield.

I hope in Thy Word.

Psalm 119: 114

Being at home gave me time to take up oil painting again and I took lessons for a while at a neighborhood art store. I was able to hold the brush in my hand now, instead of having to use my teeth, but I wasn't able to reach the top of a canvas. The only solution was to turn the canvas around and paint the top half of it upside down. Standing at a table

Sarah Margaret Smith

with the painting lying flat, was the only way I could manage all these maneuvers. Glenn, my greatest fan, insisted on framing my artistic efforts and hanging them throughout our house. I enjoyed painting but it was quite exhausting.

Some of my family from Dallas would visit from time to time. Once when my brother and his wife were with us, an unusual thing happened. Pauline was helping me get breakfast ready one morning and, having opened a can of biscuits, she was placing them in a baking pan. Suddenly, as I walked behind her toward the sink, I lost my balance and started to fall. As soon as I yelled, *"I'm falling!"* Pauline quickly turned and grabbed me with her hands up under my arms just in time. Relieved that I hadn't fallen, and everyone thankful for Pauline's quick reflexes, we finished making breakfast and sat down at the table to eat. As the food was being passed, Pauline commented, *"There are only nine biscuits here. Aren't there usually ten in a can?"* *"That's right,"* I said, *"but you know, I've been sitting here feeling I had some kind of swelling under my armpit, thinking you must have bruised me by grabbing me so hard."* Sure enough, there was the missing biscuit rising in the warmth of my underarm! We all laughed till we cried.

I loved it when Mother would come down and spend a week or so. She and Glenn got along great – she with her dry wit and he with his funny joking. She had taught me so much over the years by her example of a good wife and mother. Even her sons and daughters in law loved her dearly. Realizing she was growing old, I wanted to enjoy every moment I could with her. She related to me how she had come to faith in the Lord Jesus. I remember her reading the Bible occasionally when I still lived at home, but she never spoke about it or about the Lord. Now, it was different and we were able to share about the blessings of knowing the Savior.

102

Glenn and I with my mother

Our daughter Terri married when she was seventeen and the next year we became the grandparents of a precious little girl. Glenn and I enjoyed baby sitting little Rachel. One day she ran to greet me with a big hug, tackled me around the legs and knocked me down on the floor. *"What's the matter with Grandma?"* she asked with a puzzled look. Four years later another granddaughter, Marlena, was born. Soon after, however, Terri and her family moved to Missouri. Our younger daughter Dana went on to college but dropped out after the first year and decided to join the Navy. She studied nursing and later married a Navy man.

***

Toward the end of the 1970s, I began experiencing a weakness that prevented me from walking as far at a time as I had been able to do. When going from our bedroom to the kitchen, which was at the other end of the house, I often found myself needing to stop and lean against the wall a few minutes before I could make it the rest of the way. Walking from the parking lot into a store or restaurant was becoming difficult. Glenn and I would have to pause now and then for me to rest.

Then, we heard a news program that gave information about the condition called Post Polio Syndrome, or PPS, affecting a large percentage of polio patients even after years of improvement. *"Well, if that's what has happened to me now, it's really not so bad. So what if I'm a little slower than usual,"* I thought, unaware that PPS is usually progressive.

Several things began to come together at this time of our lives that caused us to consider making a move. First, my mother, who had been suffering with Parkinson's disease for a few years, was getting worse and I wanted to be near her; secondly, our house was not the best floor plan for my limited walking; and, thirdly, Glenn and I were both getting tired of all the traffic in Houston, as well as the high humidity. Since the girls had married and moved away, there was nothing to keep us there. I was delighted when Glenn suggested we move to the Dallas area.

Unable to find a house suited for my particular needs, we decided to buy a lot and build. Glenn gave me four weeks to design the plans. Six months later the house was completed and work was begun on the backyard pool. Family and friends helped us get unpacked and settled. Right away, Glenn found a good job as an estimator at a large construction company. Everything was working out well as we got settled and adjusted to our new surroundings.

A few days after moving in, as I was walking through the living room, I suddenly felt extremely weak and realized I could not take another step without falling. (When I fall, it's not a gentle slumping down to the floor. I crash down with full force.) I stood there a minute, holding my breath and prayed for strength to get to the nearest chair. Inching along, I finally made it and sat down. *"It's gone,"* I cried, *"My walking is gone."*

A wave of grief came over me. The twenty years of being able to walk again had gone by too fast. I thought of the nine years I struggled to reach that goal, and now it was gone. I sat there awhile under a cloud of gloom. Then, I remembered the Lord; and as quickly as the grief came, it also quickly left. God was in control of my life. Knowing that I belonged to Him, I had no reason to mourn over my condition. I needed only to trust Him and His Word.

And we know that all things work together for good to them that love God, to them who are the called according to his purpose.

Romans 8:28

Sarah Margaret Smith

> *Wait on the LORD: be of good courage,*
>
> *and he shall strengthen thine heart:*
>
> *Wait, I say, on the LORD.*
>
> *Psalm 27:14*

Comforted by His promises, I knew that He would give me the grace I needed to adjust to this new situation; and He did. Having been brought low, and then lifted by God's Word, I realized that true joy is not dependent on pleasant circumstances.

As a young girl, I tried to face my disabilities with the determination to work hard and to suppress sad thoughts. Being alone in my affliction, those were the only tools I had within myself. Now, it was quite different. In the midst of my difficulties, I knew that the Lord was upholding me, and that He had a good purpose for the trials in my life. I was confident that He would give me strength, according to His will for me. If I got better, I would praise Him. If I got weaker, by His grace and by the enablement of the Holy Spirit within me, I would still praise Him.

As Jesus told the apostle Paul,

> *My grace is sufficient for thee:*
>
> *for my strength is made perfect in weakness.*
>
> *II Corinthians 12: 9*

In the Shadow of His Hand

From then on I used my wheelchair to get from room to room, but since pushing with my feet was too exhausting, we soon bought an electric wheelchair. What a marvelous invention! It took me awhile to learn to drive without bumping into the furniture or scratching the walls, but it gave me back some of my freedom. I was able to get up out of the chair by myself and take a few steps around in the kitchen from the sink to the stove holding on to the counter. I could transfer myself from the chair to the bed with no problem. In fact, I could do almost everything at home that I did before, as long as I held on to something or someone. Going out, of course, was a different story. No longer free to walk in and out of stores, restaurants or the homes of friends, I needed my portable chair for such outings once again.

We visited with my mother and other family members often. I was delighted to live near them again after being away for fifteen years. By this time, my mother's health was going down rapidly. She lived with my brother and his wife and also had a live-in private nurse. Although she was suffering physical and mental deterioration, she had her lucid moments when we could communicate quite well. I felt very close to her during her last two years, as she often shared her thoughts and feelings with me.

As soon as it was warm enough we began going in the pool. That summer was the hottest on record for the Dallas area and we couldn't resist taking a swim almost every day. It felt great to move about freely in the water. With a swim ring around me I could go from one end of the pool to the other by kicking my legs. Thinking that my weakness was partially due to lack of exercise, I worked as hard as I could in the pool. The theory had always been "the more you do, the better you'll get." I would be exhausted afterwards but kept up the routine two or three times a week,

107

along with my usual daily activities. Since the progression of Post Polio Syndrome was intermittent and very gradual, I was unaware that I was overworking my muscles. While a slow gentle workout in the water would have been beneficial, medical research was discovering that too much exercise was counterproductive, causing permanent damage to the muscle fibers. Of course, the excessive pool exercise didn't bring on the PPS, it just sped up the progression of it. I had been overworking my muscles for a long time. Even though I was now using a wheelchair to get around the house, I continued standing too long working in the kitchen and painting at my art table. I was overusing my left arm and I wasn't resting during the day. All the while, I thought I was building up my endurance.

***

In April 1982, Glenn's company was forced to lay off many of its employees; and Glenn, being one of the newer employees, was one of them. He came home and told me the news. We wondered what the Lord had in store for us and what Glenn should do. I was beginning to need him at home, but we still needed his income. Before we even had a chance to pray about it, the phone rang. It was a realtor in Houston. She wondered if we would consider selling the acreage near Fulshear, Texas, that we had purchased as an investment several years earlier. The value had greatly increased and she had a buyer who wanted it.

Your Father knoweth what things ye have need of

before ye ask Him.

Matthew 6:8

In the Shadow of His Hand

> *My God will supply all your need according to His riches in glory in Christ Jesus.*
>
> *Philippians 4:19*

With this timely and gracious provision, Glenn was able to retire. It was wonderful having him at home. We've always enjoyed each other's company and have never understood how people get bored with retirement.

Mother was getting weaker but the doctors had not given any prognosis as to how much longer she would be with us. Every day when Glenn and I went to see her during her last hospital stay, we would stand at her bedside and Glenn would pray and read to her from the Bible. Sometimes we'd sing mother's favorite hymns and she would sing along softly with us. It seemed to comfort her. She wasn't always able to remember our names, but she remembered all the words to the hymns. One afternoon while we were there, the head nurse took me aside and suggested we spend the night. *"You do want to be with your mother when she goes, don't you?" "Of course,"* I replied. I related this to the doctor when he came by, but he said to go on home because mother could last for weeks. We decided to stay. The nurse gave us blankets and pillows and we slept on the floor in the waiting room for a couple of hours. Late that evening at mother's bedside I talked to her about the glories of heaven she would soon see. After praying and reading to her from the Scriptures, we saw her slip into a coma. Glenn left the room for a moment to speak to the nurse, and as I stood alone beside my mother, she took her last breath.

Sarah Margaret Smith

When Glenn came back into the room, we cried together and he helped me lean over to kiss my mother goodbye. An elderly woman patient in the next bed called out and asked Glenn to read again the Scriptures he had been reading aloud to mother. By then, my brother had arrived, and he read the passage to the woman while Glenn comforted me.

But I do not want you to be ignorant, brethren, concerning those who have fallen asleep, lest you sorrow as others who have no hope. For if we believe that Jesus died and rose again, even so God will bring with Him those who sleep in Jesus.

For this we say to you by the word of the Lord, that we who are alive and remain until the coming of the Lord will by no means precede those who are asleep.

For the Lord Himself will descend from heaven with a shout, with the voice of an archangel, and with the trumpet of God. And the dead in Christ will rise first. Then we who are alive and remain shall be caught up together with them in the clouds to meet the Lord in the air.

And thus we shall always be with the Lord.

Therefore comfort one another with these words.

1 Thessalonians 4: 13-18. NKJ

In the Shadow of His Hand

Knowing that mother was with the Lord and no longer in physical pain or in mental confusion, my sadness was mixed with joy. Could there be anything more wonderful than entering into eternity to be with the Lord? Of course, I would miss her but I was greatly relieved that her suffering was over.

And God shall wipe away all tears from their eyes;

and there shall be no more death, neither sorrow,

nor crying, neither shall there be any more pain:

for the former things are passed away.

Revelation 21:4

Mother's funeral was not mournful for me. Rather, it was a time of sweet reflection and gratitude for all she had been to me.

Chapter 18

Although I was forty-eight years old, it seemed strange no longer having either of my parents. My mind was rich with memories, however, and with the good counsel they had given me throughout my life. I still benefit from what I learned from them.

Life goes on, and it was time for me to find out more about how to deal with the Post Polio Syndrome that was affecting my muscles.

There were very few doctors who were informed about PPS. In fact, not many had ever worked with polio patients. The polio vaccine, discovered by Dr. Jonas Salk, had brought those epidemic years to a close in 1955. A large majority of patients that survived were now, after thirty years, beginning to experience a late-term debilitating consequence of the polio virus. It wasn't until 1983 that I found a doctor in our area, a specialist in physical medicine, who advised me correctly. He told me to rest three to four hours a day, the first thirty minutes of which I should like perfectly flat, without reading or even watching television. I was absolutely to avoid fatigue and activities that required repetitive usage of a muscle.

I read about the Dallas Area Post Polio Association that met once a month. Glenn and I went to several of the

In the Shadow of His Hand

meetings where we heard doctors and other medical professionals speak about the various aspects of PPS. There was a good amount of information given. It was explained that Polio is a virus that attacks specific neurons in the brainstem and the anterior horn cells of the spinal cord. The remaining neurons and anterior horn cells try to compensate for those that have been lost. This puts added stress on the neurons and the muscle fibers they activate. Therefore, after years of overuse, deterioration and permanent weakness occur. With all this information, I realized the importance of conserving my strength and taking care not to overwork my muscles.

Later that year I was invited to join a small group of women polio patients in our area for a monthly get-together. I assumed it was to be a time of sharing and exchanging practical ideas and information. I went to it only a couple of times because it wasn't what I expected. I've never seen the point of group therapy sessions where people sit around and describe their bitterness and hardships, but that's what this turned out to be. The old adage "misery loves company" expresses our natural bent, but indulging in such sharing for two hours seemed only to encourage self-pity. If two people are both down in a pit of despair, how can they help each other up by describing how horrible the pit is? Unless it is accompanied with positive solutions, where is the benefit? How thankful I am that at Warm Springs we were not subjected to group sessions where we could be drawn into that downward spiral of focusing on the negative. My heart broke for these women but, being new to the group, I just sat and listened.

Glenn began helping me more in the kitchen and insisted on my resting every day. I still painted some but limited my time at the art table. Glenn had no problem finding things to do in his retirement. Being a good golfer,

113

Sarah Margaret Smith

he enjoyed having more time to be out on the links. However, I was surprised when he decided we should buy a piano and that I should teach him. My first thought was, *"Oh no, this won't last."* But he stuck with it and did really well, considering his hands are like baseball mitts. Although I was still doing the cooking, Glenn decided he would learn how to make biscuits from scratch — no quick mix for him. Enthusiastic about his new hobbies, Glenn would go back and forth from the kitchen to the piano while the biscuits were baking. I'm surprised we didn't end up with biscuit dough on the piano keys! He shamed some of my lady friends when he accomplished making delicious apple pies with wonderful flaky crusts, also from scratch. I discovered that I'd married a man with many talents.

We were happy when Glenn's niece Judy and her husband and children moved up from Houston. They have been with us through thick and thin, through hospital stays and surgeries, always a joy to be with and always ready to help when we've needed them. I began teaching piano to their 13-year-old daughter Kelly, and soon her younger sister Katie gave it a try for a while. It was good to have piano back in my life. I enjoyed teaching and had fun composing music, mostly duets, for my students.

***

The travel bug bit us in the mid-80s. We went to Jamaica and Canada, as well as to Chicago, Los Angeles and San Francisco. We spent three weeks in Hawaii where we visited with our daughter Dana and her husband who was stationed there, and took a cruise out of Honolulu to the various islands. Our next trip was a cruise to Alaska. Having been carried on and off of planes, ships, trains and buses, I had become a seasoned traveler.

With these trips under our belts, we decided to tackle Europe. We took our niece Kelly with us, who by then had turned sixteen. We flew to London first, and from there we rented a car and drove out to the Cotswolds where we stayed in a quaint little country inn. Meals were served most elegantly in a small dining room. That first evening at dinner, like typical Texans, we ordered iced tea. When the waiter looked a little startled, Glenn asked him, *"You do know how to make iced tea, don't you?"* *"Of course, sir,"* he replied. But when our food was served, there was no tea. *"What about the tea?"* Glenn asked the waiter. *"Well, sir, it has to chill, you know."* After a few minutes the waiter brought three coffee cups and a large bowl filled with ice. In the middle of the ice sat a teapot of hot tea! After that, we knew not to order iced tea.

We flew on to Amsterdam, rented another car and drove on down through Switzerland and Germany. While in Munich we heard the news about terrorist attacks in several European cities. Concerned but not really afraid, we flew from Munich to Athens. We were met by two Greek airport attendants who brought the wheelchair up the stairs of the plane to me. As soon as I sat down, the 180 pound stewardess, like a middle linebacker, pushed Glenn aside and the two 120 pound airport attendants grabbed hold of the chair. Despite Glenn's protests, the men insisted they could get me down the steps. Instead of letting the chair roll down one step at a time, the little man on the front end was carrying almost all the weight of the chair and me. I prayed he would make it without having a heart attack. Once on the ground, the exhausted little man rushed me across the tarmac. Much to Glenn's dismay, he and Kelly were not allowed to come along. They were escorted through a security check while I was taken to the lower level of the airport terminal building. I wondered how I would ever find

Sarah Margaret Smith

them. The little man pushed me into a freight elevator which was to take us up to the baggage area, but suddenly the elevator stopped halfway up. Slightly exasperated, he pounded on the door yelling for help while he pushed every button, and at the same time tried to convince me everything was okay. But no one came to our rescue. After jumping up and down and jostling the elevator from side to side, he finally got the elevator working again and we made it to the main level. I wondered if Glenn by this time had notified the FBI, thinking I had been taken hostage. When we exited the elevator there was a mass of people waiting to get their luggage and go through customs. Thankfully, Glenn and Kelly had made their way over to the elevator, and found me there. Glenn took over pushing me, determined not to let me out with his sight again, and the little man went ahead to run interference for us. About that time we heard men shouting almost in unison and people began rushing frantically toward the main entrance of the terminal. *"This is it,"* we thought. *"It's a terrorist attack!"* Even though it seemed better to back away rather than to go toward the disturbance, we had no choice as the crowd was pushing us along. The little man waved his arms and shouted at people in front of us to let us go ahead. *"What is going on?"* I yelled at him. *"Don't worry, don't worry,"* he replied. *"It's just the soccer team and all the fans are here to welcome them."* What a relief!

We enjoyed our stay in Greece. It had been twenty-three years since I had seen my relatives there. It was an emotional reunion, and they were happy to meet Glenn and Kelly. Setting aside their own work schedules, they devoted their time to seeing that we were honored and entertained. Every day of our two weeks there was like a celebration with music, singing and lots of food.

Strange as it seems to us Americans, the Greeks have the habit of turning the head to the side to indicate "yes,"

116

In the Shadow of His Hand

and tilting the head up with raised eyebrows to indicate "no." These two head motions being opposite in their meaning to our way, caused confusion at times. Trying to communicate, but not knowing the language, Glenn and Kelly unthinkingly would give the wrong head motion. For example, after eating a huge meal, they would be offered more food. They would shake their heads, trying to say "no," but the hostess would happily set another full plate in front of them!

When we said our goodbyes, my uncle loaded us down with several 2-liter plastic Coke bottles filled with olive oil, made from his own olive trees. An unusual going away gift, but well appreciated!

Once again, it was time to board another airplane. This time Glenn stayed with me. He wasn't about to let anyone else push me out across the tarmac, but Kelly was taken through a security check. Instead of letting us go up the steps of the huge 747 where the other passengers were boarding, the airport attendant led us around to the other side of the aircraft. There were no steps, but a huge fork lift had just finished loading on the kitchen equipment. We were ushered up to the forklift and told to get on. *"Oh, no! Do we have to go up this way?"* I asked. *"Don't worry, don't worry,"* the man said. We rode up on a slanted metal platform that was open on three sides. Glenn was holding on to my chair with all his strength for fear I would roll off the end of the sloping platform. It was anything but a smooth ride up but we finally reached the door of the plane. We located our seats and as the engines were revving up, Glenn went up and down the aisles frantically searching until he found Kelly who was the last passenger to board. As we should have expected, it was another memorable airport experience.

Chapter 19

At home again, life took a gentler pace. Glenn and Kelly continued with their interest in piano and along with their lessons I spent much of my time writing. Mother had left me her beautiful hand-painted desk and I took up the same habit she had of sitting there jotting down thoughts, sometimes putting them in poetic form.

My Mother's Desk

Adorned with painted flowers and a soft blue scroll, with bands of gold leaf
trimming its French design,
It entered our home like a long-awaited guest, 'though purchased quite discretely at an
undisclosed price.
It was My Mother's Desk.

It took its place by the window in our formal living room. No other setting would do
for such an exquisite piece.
The small chair stood beside it when not in use, conceding to a lesser prominence than that
of My Mother's Desk.

In the Shadow of His Hand

*Three miniature drawers and space below for paper, pens and
such were hidden when the escritoire was closed,
concealing the varied contents so often in a mess. The key
remained conveniently in the lock, yet reminding one and all
that this was Mother's Desk.*

*I saw her often laboring there in a tizzy of frustration, fumbling
through household bills, searching for receipts.
But at times she seemed transported to another place and time
as she wrote her secret thoughts,
while sitting at Her Desk.*

*I find it strange to claim ownership of my inherited treasure
'though it's been in my possession for over twenty years.
For while I sit there writing, engrossed as I might be, my thoughts
are ever drawn back in lasting memory that
this was My Mother's Desk.*

– S. M. Smith

Toward the end of the 1980s, Glenn and I heard of a
senior retirement resort in the Texas Hill Country called *The
Island on Lake Travis*. After visiting it we decided to lease
an apartment there for one year, just to see how we would
like living in a retirement facility. The place was lovely and
was built out on the lake with a causeway connecting it to
the shore. Our two-bedroom apartment, or villa as it was
called, was spacious and had a balcony that faced out over
the water. I was able to get around in my electric wheelchair
to all parts of the huge complex. There were lots of activities
and while Glenn was playing golf, I attended a morning
exercise class and a watercolor class. Often I would sit
outside to read or do some sketching. I enjoyed the freedom
of being able to be out and about on my own, visiting with
neighbors or shopping at the commissary. We drove to
Austin each Sunday for church and also attended a midweek
Bible study.

Even though I was 55 and Glenn was 61, we felt like youngsters compared to the majority of the residents at The Island who were seventy and above. Regardless, we enjoyed meeting the many people there from all walks of life. One of the residents, Mr. Bailey, was a retired choral director. After meeting him, Glenn and I came up with the idea that many of the residents would probably enjoy singing together. We persuaded him to be the director if we got a group together. At least forty people signed up and before long we were singing for special programs there at The Island.

Thinking that singing would be good exercise for my breathing and limited lung capacity, I put everything I had into it. Actually, my voice did get stronger over the next several months and I was singing better than I had ever sung before. Mr. Bailey asked me to sing a solo at the upcoming Christmas program. Only a week before, Glenn and I had sung a duet during practice and I had no problem projecting my voice, and I was eager to sing praises to the Lord. When I went over the Christmas music, however, suddenly my voice became weak and I couldn't get the notes out without it cracking. It never occurred to me that I was causing permanent damage by singing so much. Even after several days and weeks of letting my voice rest, I never got it back enough to sing other than very softly and within limited range.

By the time our year was up at *The Island*, we were ready to come home. Living there had been like being on a long vacation, but now it was time to get back to real life. We had missed being at home with family and around people of all ages, instead of just the elderly.

It was becoming apparent that cooking and working in the kitchen were too much for me, but Glenn, like a trooper, took over the task without batting an eye. He even enjoyed inviting friends over and serving a delicious five

In the Shadow of His Hand

course meal. He was much better at cooking for company than I had ever been. Meanwhile, I began doing more painting in watercolor. Because my neck muscles were getting weaker, Glenn rigged up a strange looking sling that hung by a rope from the ceiling above my art table. I would place my chin in the sling which held most of the weight of my head, alleviating the strain on my neck muscles. It was a weird looking apparatus, but it helped.

Being home bodies, Glenn and I rarely went out on a weeknight, except for church services on Wednesday evenings. One Tuesday evening, however, we went to a special meeting at church held in one of the class rooms. As soon as we got there, Glenn stood before the group and opened the meeting in prayer. He then came and sat down beside me. Suddenly, he fell over unconscious. He was not breathing and had no pulse. Two men immediately began giving him CPR, while others prayed in small groups as we waited for the ambulance. I was in a state of bewilderment at what was happening, and feared that I was going to lose my beloved husband. Several women gathered around me, praying and imploring the Lord to spare Glenn's life. I wasn't even hearing all they were saying, but in a moment, a profound sense of peace came over me. It was almost as if the Lord had his arms around me, assuring me of His love for me and for Glenn, and I knew without a doubt that the whole event was in God's hands. Whether my husband would live or die I did not know, but I knew the Lord would do what was best for us.

Be not afraid of sudden fear

... for the Lord shall be thy confidence.

Proverbs 3:25-26

Meanwhile, Glenn was not coming around and, having worked over him well over five minutes, the men were about to give up, thinking there was no use to continue the CPR. But one of them, our dear friend Dennis Murphy, decided they should keep it up more vigorously. In a few minutes just as the ambulance arrived, Glenn began to revive. Accompanied by many friends to the hospital, I waited to hear the diagnosis. I marveled at God's providence in having us at a meeting that Tuesday night where other people would be around us. Had we been at home, as we normally would have been, I probably would have thought Glenn had fallen asleep in his recliner. But even if I'd been aware that he was unconscious, I wouldn't have been able to get help in time to give him CPR. I marveled, also, at God's exact timing of the incident. Had it happened fifteen minutes earlier while we were speeding down the freeway, we would have had a terrible car wreck, probably killing ourselves and others.

As Glenn was about to be rushed in for exploratory surgery, two of our church elders prayed over him. Then, Glenn reached for my hand. *"I love you,"* he said tenderly, *"and if I don't make it, I'll see you in heaven. I'm not afraid."* The surgery showed that the rigorous CPR, while it had saved his life, had caused internal bleeding. Also, the doctors confirmed that Glenn had suffered cardiac arrest due to a malfunction of his aorta valve. We learned that only a very small percentage of people live through such an experience.

The outpouring of love from family and friends gave us much encouragement. Our daughter Terri immediately came in town to help out with her dad and to stay with me while he was in the hospital. Her help was invaluable. Later, Dana came, and for the first time in years we had both our daughters with us.

In the Shadow of His Hand

The next step was for Glenn to have open-heart surgery to replace the defective aorta valve with a mechanical one, and to have a double bypass. This couldn't be done until he was completely healed from the exploratory surgery. So, we waited for three weeks, all the while praying his defective aortic valve would continue working sufficiently until the surgery.

Waiting is often the most difficult part of a trial. Anxious thoughts and questions pop into the mind, and the tendency is to engage in the worthless activity of worrying. Thankfully, the surgery went well and after thirty eight days in the hospital, Glenn was able to come home.

Chapter 20

Dana decided to come back that summer to stay with us a few months. She was always upbeat and with her funny personality, she kept us laughing. However, she had separated from her husband, and in one of our serious talks together she admitted that she was confused and lonely. Several years before, she had confessed to us that she had become addicted to prescription drugs. She was very remorseful and told us she was undergoing treatment at a rehabilitation center. Over the years she had her ups and downs, but now she was drug-free and looking forward to getting back with her husband and children. Sadly, she was being bombarded with a lot of psychological nonsense at the rehab centers. They tried to convince her that she had an inner child that was innocent, pure, beautiful and wonderful. That inner child, supposedly, was herself and was living somewhere deep down inside, wanting to come out. They tried to convince her that outside influences had caused her to do wrong things. Dana was smart enough to see the foolishness of such an idea and finally realized she had to take responsibility for her actions.

She had driven down to Texas in an old jalopy of a car which fell apart a few weeks after she arrived. While she was wondering about getting it repaired, Glenn surprised her with a brand new Chevrolet Malibu. As if she were still a young teenager, Glenn gave her all kinds of instructions about driving carefully before she left Dallas. Dana's husband had described her some years back as being the only one who could put on eye makeup, eat a taco, drink a diet Coke and nurse a baby while driving a car! That was our Dana, flighty and sometimes childlike, yet she endeared herself to everyone who knew her. She returned to California where her husband was stationed, and was happy being a wife and mother again. At last, everything seemed to be going well with her and we kept in close contact. She started going to church, taking her children with her. However, because of all she had put her family through, feelings of guilt continued to come over her periodically. To alleviate her depression the doctors were quick to put her on a strong antidepressant. Sadly, the drug had an opposite effect on her.

On the morning of March 11, 1995, Dana took her own life. Losing a child is a devastating heartbreak. Even though I was only her stepmother, I loved her dearly. Rarely a day goes by that I don't think of her.

I have grieved over the death of my stepdaughter, in addition to the deaths of my parents, my older brother, my older sister, a brother-in-law and a nephew. Each of these close family members had a special place in my heart. The greatest comfort to me in times of grief and in times of suffering has been in knowing that the Lord is righteous and in sovereign control over all the events of our lives. He allows illness and tragedy to touch us for purposes we may not always understand. But that's where faith comes in, and its genuineness is proven.

... that the trial of your faith, being much more precious than gold that perisheth, though it be tried with fire, might be found unto praise and honor and glory at the appearing of Jesus.

1 Peter 1:7

A long life is sure to have its sorrows as well as its pleasures. I have had many joyful blessings and happy times, for which I'm grateful. However, it has not been so much during the happy times that my trust in the Lord has deepened, but during the difficult times. Just as shadows give dimension to a painting, so struggles and hardships often help us to appreciate the beauty around us, and to realize the faithfulness of God. More importantly, trials help us to grow, and God uses them to cultivate within us a needed perspective in regard to life and eternity. They remind us of our constant need for Divine help. The more I see my frailties, the more I see Christ as my strength.

Chapter 21

Time is such a precious commodity. I never appreciated it when I was young. In our youth we want time to pass quickly; not realizing it gives us the space we need in which to grow, to learn and sometimes to heal. A time of healing from sorrow enables us to move on and enjoy life once again, hopefully with a deeper sense of the value of time and the importance of not squandering it.

We are instructed in the Scriptures that we are to "redeem the time." It doesn't say to redeem the time *unless you have a physical disability*; so, I had to conclude that the exhortation was for me, as much as for others. But what does it mean to redeem the time? In summing up what I read in the commentaries, I found it means that we are to value the time that God has given us and use it for good purposes, as a service unto Him. That's a tall order when there are so many diversions constantly pulling at us.

Time

O, Time, I walk within your measured frame,
knowing not the number of my days.
Too often I have wasted, to my shame,
this gift of God so graciously ordained.

Sarah Margaret Smith

And yet I do not own your passing span,
nor can I reach and hold you in my hand.
Enjoyed or endured, but never grasped,
the present slips away to form the past.

But I would never ask you to remain
nor suddenly reverse your onward flow,
for hope inspires my heart toward each new day
as God's purposes for me in Time unfold.
– S. M. Smith

Feeling rather useless since my kitchen duties had been taken from me, I began to pray every day for the Lord to show me how I could serve Him. My painting was an enjoyable pastime but I could hardly classify it as a service unto the Lord. In my Bible reading I was struck by the exhortation in Titus Chapter 2, which states that older women are to teach the younger women in matters pertaining to being a godly woman, a godly wife and a godly mother. I had read the Bible passage many times over the years and had benefited personally from encouragements from older women. My first mentor, of course, was my mother who had much practical wisdom. I also learned about child discipline from my older sisters as I watched them train their children to be well behaved. After that, the woman in Houston who led the Bible study on the Christian home pointed out to me the scriptural references that give instruction for godly living and explain the important role of wives and mothers.

But how in the world could I follow the Lord's instruction to encourage the younger women? I saw other older women reaching out to them, but I felt inadequate, since I was physically the least capable of being a good wife

In the Shadow of His Hand

and mother. I had never even kept house, washed a load of clothes or ironed my husband's shirts. I had never borne nor raised a child from infancy. Part of me wanted to forget about the exhortation, wrap myself up in my excuse of being disabled and watch others minister to them. After praying about it and looking for the Lord's direction, it came to me that while participating in the activities of life is normally the best way to learn, it is also true that observation from the sidelines can teach us, albeit from a different perspective. In spite of my limitations and hesitations, the Lord had brought into my life several young married women, some whose mothers lived far away. I would visit with them after church or they would call seeking advice. I couldn't get away from the fact that a needed ministry was there. Most of them had young children and had little time for fellowship with other young mothers. The thought came to me that a morning class once or twice a month could bring these young women together for some biblical instruction and for a time of sharing. I was driven to the Scriptures to study over and over the exhortations given pertaining to the Christian home, and to learn about the lives of godly women in the Bible. With much prayer and with Glenn's guidance, I prepared an outline for several lessons. Thus, the "Titus 2 Class," as we called it, began meeting in our home.

Chris convinced us that I needed a computer complete with software that would type out my words as I dictated into a microphone. Glenn and I were fascinated with the amazing technology as I was able to put the lessons in print and not exhaust my left hand by writing or trying to type.

The Lord even provided a babysitter, through the generosity of one of our church members, to watch all the little children in the back room while we women crowded around the dining room table with our Bibles and notebooks.

129

Studying and learning together, and getting to know these young women, was a special blessing for me. As the class grew, I invited other older women to teach on occasion.

After several years of leading the class, I realized my voice wasn't strong enough to keep it up. Another woman willingly took over and began having the class in her home. I still keep in touch with many of the young women. A few of them take turns coming over once a week to help me with personal care, including, massages, pedicures, etc. Other ladies from the church bring meals, in order to give Glenn a break from having to cook everyday. How sweet to see God's love being manifested through them in these special ways!

A few of the young women and I have started a summer homemaking class for their daughters, who are now teenagers. The girls are instructed by the "grandmas" of our church in social etiquette, sewing, needlework and cooking. I'm mostly behind the scenes in this project, but I like watching the young girls working enthusiastically as they interact with the older ladies. It has been a ministry, both to the young and to the old.

Teaching piano is still part of my life. Kelly took lessons until she graduated from high school and now that she's married with lots of children, three of her daughters are my students. After their lessons they lovingly help with household chores. We eat lunch and then have a time to sing songs, play games or do crafts.

Although I never had children of my own, the Lord has fulfilled that desire in me by giving me beautiful stepchildren, grandchildren, great-grandchildren, nieces and nephews. The young women friends the Lord has brought into my life are like daughters, as well.

He maketh the barren woman to keep house,
and to be a joyful mother of children.

Psalm 113:9

With increased weakness in my left hand, I've had to put away the paintbrushes. Amazingly, the more the effects of post polio weaken me, the more the Lord provides me with new projects and purposes. I was happy to discover new software for my computer that would enable me to write music. Just by clicking the mouse I can place notes where I want them on the music staff, and then play them back to hear what I have written. I never knew that a little "mouse" would be such a helpful companion! It's almost like being able to play the piano again after fifty years. Now, with minimum physical exertion I'm able to write hymns and other piano music.

I've learned that no matter how old or how weak one might be, there's always something worthwhile to do, whether it's taking time to read to a little child or to telephone someone who is sick. As we focus on the Lord and on the needs of others, we are less burdened by our own afflictions. Praying for others is certainly an important ministry that we Christians can do even when we are at our weakest. There's no reason to feel useless.

In spite of my resting every afternoon, I was still fatigued and often short of breath. Sometimes at night I experienced a form of apnea. I would wake up startled, gasping for air. I went to see a lung specialist who tested my breathing and found it to be less than fifty percent of normal. He ordered a ventilator for me to use each night.

Glenn straps the mask on my face and the automatic pumping of air into my lungs gives my breathing muscles eight hours of needed rest. Also, another breathing machine was ordered for me to use twenty minutes twice a day. In less than a week of using the machines I noticed improvement in my breathing and in my speaking ability. I began sleeping better and feeling more energized. How wonderful sleep is! It recuperates both body and mind.

My nighttime sleep, even with the ventilator, is usually interrupted long before dawn, and I spend a couple of hours enjoying the silence during those wee hours of the early morning. I treasure that intervening period of time in which I can lie there in the quiet and think, pray and plan for the day. It's also my favorite time for composing songs and piano music. I sing the words and hear the notes over and over in my mind even after I go back to sleep. As soon as I can get to my computer in the morning, my mouse and I write them down.

Since taking a bad fall one day in 2004, I'm no longer able to get up out of my wheelchair or in and out of bed by myself. This latest loss of independence has been one of the hardest adjustments for me to make since PPS struck me, because it puts even more responsibility on Glenn. He helps me with almost everything now and, yet, he does it all willingly. He has given up so much for me, but in spite of that, our love grows deeper year by year. He is a most wonderful husband. His sacrificial love for me is truly an example and a picture of Christ's love for the church, and fulfills the exhortation in God's Word:

Husbands, love your wives,

even as Christ also loved the church,

and gave Himself for it.

Ephesians 5:25

One time, a newly married young lady asked me if she should be expected to pick up her husband's wet towels after he showers. Immediately, a lump came into my throat and tears filled my eyes. *"Oh, my dear,"* I replied, *"be ever so thankful that you can do even such small things as that for your husband. It's a privilege for a wife who loves her husband to wait on him. There may come a time when you can't, and you will wish you could."*

To Glenn
The love we share is like the sun –
It keeps away the cold of loneliness.
It brightens even the gray of winter's drabness.
It shines upon my heart when weariness
would steal from me the smile of happiness.
And like the sun our love endures
through stormy clouds that would obscure
its constant arms of golden rays –
Beams of warmth, still there awaiting
opportunities for proclaiming,
each day anew,
the love we share.

– S. M. Smith

Chapter 22

About six months after I came down with polio, my Mother wrote a poem she called *Promise Me Not – (Margaret's Song)*. However, she waited several years before showing it to me. Even though by then I had moved away from home, was working and trying to live as independently as possible, I found the poem extremely difficult to read. As I read, I saw in it the secret sadness of a young girl – and I remembered being that young girl. A surge of long-suppressed emotion welled up within me and I couldn't bear its reality. It was too painful. I put the poem away and dismissed it from my mind. Just recently I discovered it in a box of mementos I had tucked away almost forty years ago.

In the Shadow of His Hand

Promise Me Not –
This is Margaret's song.

Promise me not a chariot. Just let my feet tread ground
green with grass once more –
To feel the breath of wind caress me as each glad step breaks the
still air—each step a glorious journey, links in a golden chain, to
take me everywhere.

Promise me not a tapestried cushioned chair, but the mossy
earthbound roots of a spreading tree to sit upon –
A sandy beach beside a lake, a wooden picnic bench or, better still,
the doorsteps of home.

Promise me not exotic flowers – I'd love to stoop and pick a
dandelion; I'd strip the young leaves from a tender branch, and
breathe in the fragrance of the green petaled flower they make in
my hand.

Promise me not security just of gold – my heart needs love of
loved ones – shoulders strong enough to bear my bended head,
and willing hands to catch my falling tears, shed in sorrow for
these lost years.

Promise me not music renowned. For, Oh! My fingers ache to
touch the keys
with pressure just enough to run the scales or strike a simple chord.
Then I know, I know, the music in my heart would be echoed in
my fingertips.

Promise me not a promise of "things." But promise me a promise
not of less than the promise of happiness.

– by Ola Brockles
January 27, 1951

Now as I read her poem, I see much more in it than I did before. It no longer saddens me, but I am moved by my mother's insight, her empathy, her compassion, her pain and her understanding heart. I see that her suffering was far greater than my own. Thankfully, the longings of that young girl are now understood from the context of God's wise and merciful providence for me. I'm grateful for the life He gave me. I've needed, evidently, to go through a crucible of trials in order to learn, and I'm still learning, to cling more closely to Him and to wait confidently on His promises. Above all, I'm thankful that the Lord saved me, gave me new life in Christ and the faith to trust in Him.

The poem was "my song," as Mother described it, but only for a period of time. My song is quite different now. Would I not like to walk in the grass, to pick a flower, to play the piano? Of course, I would. But while such things would be enjoyable, I've learned that they are not the basis of fulfillment or of true happiness. My mother prayed I would find happiness and by God's grace I have. He gave me a loving husband, a beautiful marriage, children, a comfortable home, close friends and much more. These are truly wonderful blessings, but even these, because they are only temporal, can't give peace or rest to the soul. Only Christ can do that. He is the greatest gift and He alone fulfills and provides the peace that lasts forever. Whether my circumstances are hard or pleasurable, knowing Christ Jesus as my Lord and my Savior is the essence, the basis and the sum and substance of true joy. I thank God for redeeming me, for forgiving me of my sins and for adopting me as His own blood-bought child.

In the Shadow of His Hand

Thanks be to God for His unspeakable gift!

2 Corinthians 9:15

And He hath put a new song in my mouth, even

praise unto our God!

Psalm 40: 3

If you would you like to purchase
In the Shadow of His Hand
please visit the publisher's bookstore at
www.E-BookTime.com

Available in paperback and hardcover editions.

Printed in the USA
CPSIA information can be obtained
at www.ICGtesting.com
JSHW020002290324
60079JS00001B/58